America's
Historic Landscapes

America's Historic Landscapes

Community Power and the Preservation of Four National Historic Sites

Ary J. Lamme III

The University of
Tennessee Press
KNOXVILLE

Copyright © 1989 by The University of Tennessee Press / Knoxville.
All Rights Reserved. Manufactured in the United States of America.
First Edition.

The paper in this book meets the minimum requirements
of the American National Standard for Permanence
of Paper for Printed Library Materials.
∞
The binding materials have been chosen
for strength and durability.

Library of Congress Cataloging in Publication Data

Lamme, Ary J., 1940–
    America's historic landscapes : community power
and the preservation of four national historic sites /
Ary J. Lamme III. — 1st ed.
        p.   cm.
    Bibliography: p.
    Includes index.
    ISBN 0-87049-614-X (cloth: alk. paper)
    1. National parks and reserves—United States.
2. Historic sites—United States—Conservation and
restoration.   3. Landscape protection—United States.
4. Landscape—United States.   I. Title.
E160.L36 1989
363.6'9—dc20   89-4925   CIP

For my Family

Contents

Figures

Preface

As a young boy I enjoyed picnics on the battlefield at Gettysburg. At that time my family lived in Westminster, a small town in Western Maryland. Baltimore and Gettysburg were both about thirty miles away. When friends visited, or even if the family was just looking for a pleasant diversion, we often chose to make a trip to that historic landscape rather than to a metropolitan area.

What was the attraction of Gettysburg? I have often asked myself that question in later years, as I developed a geographers' professional interest in the interaction of humans with environments. Taking my family as reasonably representative members of the general public, I have consciously tried to analyze in retrospect how we felt when we were unself-consciously enjoying Gettysburg.

There are certainly many aspects of Gettysburg that are appealing. These include an attractive physical setting—a pleasant town in southern Pennsylvania—recreational facilities at the national park, interesting and informative exhibits, and the site of a momentous historical event. My favorite battlefield site was called "Devil's Den." It is an area filled with large boulders, and it lies across a small valley from Little Round Top. Here Confederate sharpshooters placed pressure on the left end of Union lines that ran along Cemetery Ridge. Descriptive signs at Devil's Den included what seemed to be post-battle pictures. Later I learned that a number of those pictures had been posed by photographer Matthew Brady and his assistants. So part of my image of that location was false, but it was nevertheless an operative image that had power for me.

Martial interests constituted only a small portion of my attraction to Gettysburg. For several years running in school we were taught to recite the Gettysburg address, and the site at which that speech was originally delivered in the National Cemetery, among symmetrical rows of headstones and markers with poems to the fallen, was a focal point of my excursions. Through booklets and exhibitions at Gettysburg I got a partial glimpse of what mid-nineteenth-century life in a small town must have been like and an appreciation for the larger sociopolitical currents of that time.

Mostly, however, Gettysburg just seemed to be a great place for a family outing. My father was commuting on weekends from New York City, and it was a good opportunity to spend some time with him. Then, too, is there any better place to eat a peanut butter and jelly sandwich than on top of a giant boulder with a grand panorama in view?

At that time I thought of Gettysburg as a mid-nineteenth-century place. The park's historic landscapes were the objects of my attention, and I somehow assumed that time stood still on the battlefield. Everything else—modern roads, visitor facilities, and even the town—seemed subservient to that landscape. Even today I cling to my childhood, family-associated, image of Gettysburg. Down deep I know that this simplistic belief in the subservience of all interests to the primacy of a historic landscape is not reality. The battlefield is not as it was in the 1860s. Further, concern for the integrity of that landscape is not a fundamental tenet in the minds of many who have power over it.

While some of my thoughts about Gettysburg are meaningful only to me, some images I share with large numbers of the American public. My conviction that individual experience in places like Gettysburg is universally important and needs to be planned for has stimulated the research projects that culminated in this book.

Many people have helped me along the way. Secondary school instruction by Raymond Oliver and Paul Carre at McDonogh School in Maryland gave me exposure to and confidence in the mathematical and social sciences. I was fortunate enough to have a high-quality undergraduate education at Principia College. There geographer George Knadler, historian James Belote, and English professor Colin Campbell prompted me to develop and use important scholarly tools. Many small liberal arts colleges have great scholars on their faculties, and Principia is no exception. Charles B. Hosmer, Jr., is internationally recognized as a preservation historian. Chuck Hosmer shared many files from the preparation of his classic *Preservation Comes of Age* and generously spent time discussing matters related to the preservation of historic landscapes. English professor Peter E. Martin, my Principia classmate, has communicated his thought-provoking humanistic views of landscape to me in correspondence covering many years.

In a similar way, my graduate work was an important step toward this study. Joseph Russell at the University of Illinois helped me enter Syracuse University for doctoral work when I was unexpectedly released from the Air Force during the Vietnam era. At Syracuse, David Sopher and Donald Meinig were constantly stimulating and encouraging mentors whose understanding of landscapes has set a high standard for many of us.

A number of people associated with the sites studied in this book have provided me with materials and information. Superintendent Richard H. Maeder of Colonial National Historical Park has patiently answered my questions and arranged for me to receive materials from his library. Park Historian Kathleen Georg Harrison of Gettysburg National Military Park shared her views and materials. Daniel J. Palm, Director of the St. Lawrence–Eastern Ontario Commission and resident of Sackets Harbor has told me of his perspective on that site. Marcia Osterhout, who was involved in Sackets Harbor preservation, has given me information on the current situation. Gail Meyer Kuriger, a former resident of Sackets Harbor, shared material about archeological studies. My long-time friend, Douglas B. McDonald, Deputy Director of the Bridge and Port Authority at Ogdensburg, New York, has patiently gathered Sackets Harbor material for my use.

Stephen H. Rogers, Staff Cartographer at the Department of Geography, University of Florida, has been extremely diligent in producing high quality graphics for the text. Political scientists Bert Swanson and William Kelso have discussed their insights on community power. Alachua County Planner William Kinser has shared the fascinating story of Cross Creek.

A family man cannot possibly undertake this kind of an effort without the support of those he loves. My parents and sister were the companions of my early years at Gettysburg and Williamsburg. My wife, Linda Leonard Lamme, has graciously taken time away from her own distinguished academic endeavors to allow me those all-important extra hours. Laurel, my daughter, has been a wonderful companion on field trips to several of the study sites. Ary IV loves to romp in historic landscapes, giving them added meaning to me.

For all this assistance I am very grateful. Of course, I accept full responsibility for this work.

America's
Historic
Landscapes

1. Introduction

Smelling wood smoke, hearing the footfalls of marching cadets, savoring the taste of ethnic cooking, feeling the light touch of a sea breeze—all these sensations help us to fully conceptualize places like a New England campsite, the parade ground at West Point, a festival on the Eastern Shore of Maryland, and the beach at Sanibel Island. We use all our senses to comprehend such places in our environment, and, while sensing, we are simultaneously assigning meaning to those places.

Every scene that we sense has meaning in our lives. The multifaceted scenes of home, of neighborhood, of community, of employment and other human activities are constant companions and points of reference that enable us to carry on our human affairs. These are the homescapes, townscapes, and landscapes of our lives. Different settings make us feel differently. We may be comfortable at home or visiting family and friends, awed at a grand natural scene, proud at a parade, and so ill-at-ease in the presence of urban blight that we avoid its presence. The landscapes we sense and the meanings we attach to that sensing are individual. Yet, environmental perception is an experience shared by all people.

In fact, some landscapes have acquired extraordinary status because their symbolic meaning is so widely shared. "Certain settings . . . have such a strong 'spirit of place' that they will tend to have a similar impact on many different people. The Grand Canyon or the left bank of the Seine in Paris are excellent examples" (Steele 1981, 9). Human action and reaction at such places resides permanently in public consciousness, whether the landscape in question is a local park, whose impact is confined to a small public, or a nationally recognized setting. Using the word "historic" to describe these landscapes denotes their frequent association with events of the past as well as the magnitude of their fame. These extraordinary places are the objects of this study.

Visiting Historic Landscapes

Historic landscapes are part of the experience of most people, and millions visit them each year. Local sites associated with town pioneers, striking buildings, or scenes of natural beauty are generally easy to reach and pull local traffic. Historic landscapes of national renown draw visitors from a wider area. Many travel considerable distances to seek out specific sites, and they arrive with high expectations. People from all classes and backgrounds come to these extraordinary places, and no special talent is required to enjoy them. However, one thing is essential for people to experience historic landscapes—free time. With more time available to more people, historic sites in the United States are experiencing ever-increasing numbers of visitors.

Increased discretionary time is a reflection of changes in our society. A "broad and growing humanistic ethic in the United States" is making the availability of reasonable amounts of leisure time a national requirement (Grey and Greber 1979). Changes such as the movement toward a thirty-six-hour or four-day work week mean more opportunity for recreation (Lazer 1982). Better retirement programs financed by employers as well as employees place more disposable income in individual hands. These funds permit a greater variety of free-time activities.

Most of us have, use, and spend money on discretionary time. An analysis and projection of time spent in discretionary activities in the United States during the twentieth century indicates the growing importance of this time to Americans (Holman 1961). Looking at the years 1900, 1950, and 2000, Holman estimated total hours spent in various activities. The percentage of time allocated to required activities such as sleep, work, school, housekeeping and personal care came out to 73.5, 65.9, and 61.9 for those three years. Time spent on discretionary activity amounted to 26.5, 34.1, and 38.3 percent of total available hours. These estimates show a 50 percent increase since the beginning of the current century in time given to personal choice activity. Most of this increase represents time taken from employment.

A portion of most individuals' discretionary time is spent away from home. Tourist figures for the State of Florida suggest something of the national magnitude of vacation travel and spending. In 1982 approximately 40 million tourists, four times the population of the state, visited Florida and spent 21.5 billion dollars (Terhune 1983, 483–89). During the same year 14.9 million people visited Florida state parks and recreation sites. Tourist-related businesses collected $570 million dollars in state sales taxes. Over 90 percent of these visitors had been to Florida before, and approximately 95 percent said they would come again (Marth and Marth 1983, 312–14).

There are, of course, many vacation spots in the United States other than those in Florida where citizens of the United States and other developed countries can spend their increased time and money on discretionary activities. Why do they frequently use this time to travel to historic places?

Recreational Destinations

Places that people visit in the United States today are sites that have long been appealing. Because more people make these journeys, better and larger capacity facilities are necessary. However, the underlying appeal of certain types of places has been constant. The public is more sophisticated in its choice of specific recreational sites than many would have guessed (Nelson and Butler 1974). Families consider a wide range of factors when deciding on vacation destinations. In addition to personal preferences and available travel opportunities, site characteristics such as accessibility, facility availability, planned activities, and natural setting enter into the choice of a recreational destination. People are attracted by a combination of physical characteristics and cultural attributes. Most places that lure large numbers of people have many attractive features.

Theme parks like Disneyland and Sea World prosper in locations where people are used to going because of a favorable climate. Repeated tourist surveys reveal that Florida's most attractive characteristic is its natural resource base (Marth and Marth 1983, 312). People come to Florida for the climate, beaches, and wilderness parks. Without high-quality natural resources, Sea World, Disney World, and other attractions of the Sunshine State would be in trouble.

Historic sites are also traditional tourist destinations. Most people live in ordinary landscapes; that is, places whose meaning is shared with other similar places and is specifically appreciated only by a limited audience. While people have a strong attachment to their homescapes, many have shown an interest in visiting places with extraordinary natural and cultural associations. As with other recreational sites, visits to historic landscapes are increasing dramatically. Future projections suggest significant increases in visitation at each of the landscapes studied in this book. Thus, pressure mounts on the resources of historic sites. Sustaining historic landscapes is a complex process. Landscapes at historic places are not constructed; they are nurtured and preserved. Management at historic sites requires an understanding of factors that affect landscape development. This book aims to help by providing that understanding.

Goals of this Research

Abraham Lincoln, in his classic address at Gettysburg, revealed a deep appreciation for the importance of special places. The challenged and imminently triumphant Union principles of the Civil War years seemed to him to be symbolized by the battlefield cemetery. His words struck a responsive cord then and today.

> We are met on a great battlefield of that war. We have come to dedicate a portion of that field as a final resting place for those who here gave their lives that that nation might live. It is altogether fitting and proper that we should do this. But, in a larger sense, we cannot dedicate, we cannot consecrate, we cannot hallow this ground. The brave men, living and dead, who struggled here have consecrated it far above our poor power to add or detract.

Lincoln was right. We can't add or detract from symbolic meaning given to Gettysburg by those who participated in armed struggle. However, we can add, and unfortunately are more likely to detract, from elements of that landscape which positively influence public experience.

Gettysburg is extraordinary, not by design, but by universal recognition of its "sense of place" as first characterized by Lincoln. He knew that what had gone on there had meaning beyond military victory. Lincoln's recognition that the cemetery was meaningful in a larger context of national trauma explicitly conferred distinction on the entire landscape. Yet, if Gettysburg's meaning does not require human enhancement, there is a definite need for active preservation of the setting. What Lincoln could not have foreseen were threats that public utilization and rampant commercialism would pose to the sense of that place.

Experience at Gettysburg and similar places prompts the dual goals of this research: (1) to study the association of meaning and place; how places acquire meaning, the nature of that meaning, and a consequent rationale for preservation of historic landscapes; (2) to study historic landscape preservation: the patterns of power, the challenges, the institutional frameworks, and the decision-making processes at extraordinary places.

Methodology

The methods used in this analysis of the evolution of historic landscapes are based on three premises:

1. An examination of the history of landscape development at individual places reveals important characteristics of and factors affecting landscape preservation. Therefore, the case study approach is emphasized in this research.

2. Contemplative analyses of landscape meaning at selected sites suggest a range of public reactions to those places. Therefore, the study includes personal and collective reactions to particular landscapes.

3. Community power perspectives provide a plausible explanation for patterns of control over historic landscapes. Therefore, each of the study areas is analyzed in that theoretical context.

Following this introduction, chapter 2 contains a review of literature on issues related to landscape and meaning and attempts to match landscape experience with explanation. Chapter 3 reviews community power and its application to landscape management. Sources of power over landscapes are a vital concern in preservation and management. Theories of community power suggest a common source of power and provide a more systematic framework for analysis of landscape evolution.

Chapters 4 through 7 are case studies of four different sites in the eastern United States, an area that is most familiar to the author. Each landscape has attained some degree of public recognition as a site of symbolic importance. The sites were chosen purposely to represent a broad range of landscape characteristics with differing origins, physical settings, and cultural traits. In addition, each site faces a unique set of challenges. These varied characteristics allow for analyses of many different elements and situations associated with attempts to preserve and utilize historic landscapes.

St. Augustine, Florida, the subject of chapter 4, was founded during the Spanish Colonial Period in North America. It is an urban landscape with many forms of institutional control over cultural and recreational features. Varied public and private interests have produced a bewildering array of problems, some of which are attributable to differing ideas of how St. Augustine should be developed.

Colonial National Historical Park in Virginia, the focus of chapter 5, contains a variety of historic places in rural and small-town environments. These places include sites of the first permanent English settlement in the New World and of the decisive battle of America's revolution. Although not an official part of the park, Colonial Williamsburg is an important neighboring historic landscape. In this relatively limited peninsular area the challenge to create a unified historic landscape interpretation for visitors remains unfulfilled after six decades.

Sackets Harbor, New York, an important early Federal period port on the Great Lakes and later site of a major military installation is the topic of chapter 6. Its relative obscurity in recent years is traceable to the fact that effective preservation of an attractive historic landscape has eluded the best efforts of interested individuals.

Gettysburg, Pennsylvania, one of the quintessential symbolic landscapes of America, is the concluding case study in chapter 7. This small town has lived with the honor and burden of overwhelming symbolic association for over a century. The landscape elements are seemingly simple—a town and the battlefield. But lack of complexity has not eased the challenges of responsible development and management.

Chapter 8 is a review of the findings and strategies associated with the evolution of historic landscapes. I try to integrate theoretical and empirical data. Answers to questions that recur in regard to these places highlight important matters that need to be taken into consideration when one undertakes to preserve landscapes and their meaning.

The case study chapters are not complete histories or even preservation histories of each site. Particular facets of history and geography are emphasized as illustrating themes related to this research. Thus, one case study focuses on preservation efforts during the Depression while another features a chronicle of current events as citizens attempt to preserve their landscape heritage. More complete historical sources for each site are listed in the bibliography.

I don't claim to be unbiased in my concern for what I feel is appropriate preservation action. When it comes to assessment of landscape management I often state my belief that *good landscape preservation is essential for our national well-being and advantageous for all our citizens.* Within that context, every effort has been made to present an accurate account of attempts to preserve these special places.

Increased utilization of these extraordinary landscapes exerts pressure on historic resources and justifies this attempt to foster better understanding and management of them. If our families and our nation are to enjoy the advantages of historic landscapes, we need to have a clear grasp of how these places developed both physically and symbolically, and of ways to meet the significant challenges to their preservation. This study of the development of four historic sites in the eastern United States strives to provide a degree of comprehension useful to citizen, scholar, and manager.

2. Landscape and Meaning

Robert McCloskey wrote several children's books about Homer Price, a fictional ten-year-old growing up in a midwestern town (McCloskey 1943). The books are a farcical review of small-town life during the 1930s and 1940s. McCloskey's stories are hilarious to children and have special meaning for adults who share children's literature, prompting them to give second thoughts to some of the everyday aspects of human life.

Homer's town, Centerburg, was once called "Edible Fungus," a name derived from the circumstances surrounding the town's founding. Ezekial Enders, a pioneer leader, escorted settlers to the site of the town without supplies. They were saved by the discovery of fungal food. In a chapter called "Wheels of Progress," the town is about to celebrate its 150th anniversary. A celebration highlight will be a pageant featuring a theme song rendered by the church choir with these lyrics:

> Forty two pounds of edible fungus,
> In the wilderness a-growin'.
> Saved the settlers from starvation,
> Helped the founding of the nation. (153)

However, the celebration is not intended just to commemorate the past. An integral part of the festivities involves the opening of a new housing area. Homer's relative, Uncle Ulysses, runs a luncheonette on the town square with a wonderful machine that automatically produces many identically perfect doughnuts. Uncle Ulysses figures that the same principle might produce housing. He convinces a spinster descendent of the town founder to construct a housing tract on their historic landscape, the old Enders estate. All the vegetation is removed, and the land flattened. The only reminder of the estate's former use is the Victorian mansion, which remains.

As the celebration nears, mass-produced houses begin to arrive on trucks. Each home is assembled on an identical square lot, with identical furniture, and identical shrubbery outside. However, Uncle Ulysses has trouble getting street signs and numbers in place. Thus, new residents find their homes by counting in rows and columns from the old mansion. During the celebration week town leaders decide that the Victorian mansion is a sore thumb among these uniform, progressive houses. They have it taken down and replaced with a house identical to all the rest. Consequently, at the height of the celebration everyone gets lost on the way home. The answer for Centerburg is not only to add street signs and numbers but also to reconstruct the mansion. Nobody wants to take a chance on getting lost again.

Initial reaction to this tale might be that Uncle Ulysses and other town leaders are tasteless and comical fools. Converting a local historic landscape into a uniform plain is a preservationist's nightmare and would put all geographers out of work. However, this story dates from the Levittown era, when many people who had never owned a home before were suddenly able to afford a single-family dwelling. A uniform landscape of small rectangular homes seems progressive to some people—a dream come true.

What must be remembered first and foremost about landscapes is that they symbolize different things to different individuals. There are as many symbolic landscapes as there are people. All interpretations have worth. Yet, we must try to reach a generalized understanding of these places. As social scientists we push on, trying to evaluate and manage the utilization of places. We are wise to remember, however, that the foundation of landscape meaning is an individual value judgment by resident and observer, a factor that must be considered in any analysis of place.

Susan Allen Toth wrote two memoirs (1982, 1984), one dealing with her childhood years in Ames, Iowa, and the other with her experiences with higher education at two different colleges. While she terms the books "memoirs," the one set in Ames could also be called the biography of a town. Toth has also written about her experiences since publication of those books (1987). People from her past have gotten in touch to reminisce and relate their individual reactions to shared experiences, and Toth tells about a number of these encounters. A particularly meaningful one was with Angelika, the daughter of Italian immigrants who lived "beyond the railroad tracks." Toth's conclusion is that "Angelika's Ames was clearly not my quiet, middle-class, self-satisfied town."

Toth's early life is inextricably linked with place. One would not want to separate experience from place, for both are necessary to the truth. A geography of Ames must take into account the memoirs of its residents. Yet, problems of accuracy arise. She writes: "Did I tell the truth? Did the way I now feel about the past mean I'd felt the same way then? The kaleidoscope keeps turning. It can make me dizzy. Then I have to stop, put the kaleidoscope down, take a deep breath and determinedly look out the window into my present" (1987, 38). This kind of interpretation is essential to an understanding of the meaning place can carry. The challenges of working with such interpretations are simultaneously awesome and glorious.

This chapter explores the relationship of landscape and meaning through sections that define the concept of landscape, place landscape experience in a universal context, discuss the nature of human interaction with environment, and outline approaches for interpreting landscape meaning.

Defining Landscape

Landscape has been called "all that can be seen on the earth's surface from a particular place" (Larkin and Peters 1983, 139). This definition is much too limited for me. Landscape is not just the solid material features that you see as your vision stretches to the horizon. Landscape is an idea held in mind, and may not be observable.

I define landscape as *a composite image of space*. This definition means that landscape is always an integration of related parts, that it has to be a mental image to be important, and that the object of this integrative image is space along the earth's surface. Thus, there are really multitudinous landscapes of the same place—as many landscapes as there are people experiencing that place. Furthermore, when one speaks of the urban landscape, the object may be entirely a mental image and not an observable scene. In every instance, whether it is being directly observed or not, landscape refers to a mental conception of related elements in space.

My use of the word "symbolic" at various places in this text refers to the fact that as mental concepts, all landscapes must have meaning. Meinig comments: "We regard all landscapes as symbolic, as expressions of cultural values, social behavior, and individual actions worked upon particular localities over a span of time" (1979, 6). Even if landscapes possess objective reality, the search for that reality would be hopeless because the observer and the observed are so infused with value that objectivity becomes impossible.

Common or folk landscapes are relatively undistinguished, everyday places where people live, work, and play. A volume of essays devoted to interpretation of "ordinary" landscapes testifies to growing interest in this topic (Meinig 1979). Peirce Lewis's essay in that collection notes that common landscapes have suffered from scholarly neglect but are worthy of attention because of all they can tell us about the lives of us folk (19). In contrast, the adjective "historic" is used to differentiate extraordinary landscapes that are widely recognized as places possessing important symbolic images from the common landscapes of our everyday affairs. The shared symbolization of these special places is well described by Duncan's phrase as "a kind of tacit understanding among participants in a cultural system" (1985, 182).

Universality of Landscapes

Landscape is a universal component of human experience, and this universality proves to be one of landscape's advantages as a focus of research. Since landscape is shared by all people it ceases to be unique, and although interpretations of landscape may be criticized as exceptional, the subject matter and recurrent questions about landscapes cannot be dismissed on those grounds.

What are the universals of human experience? Beyond purely biological needs for survival, there are a number of common experiences. Human young would not survive without the care and nurturing provided in families, and the family remains a focus of experience for most of us throughout our lives. A second universal is the need to make or maintain a living. By that is meant the necessity to engage in productive activity to supply basic requirements for survival. Most of us meet this universal need by what we call a "job," and many of us attach a great deal of importance to this segment of our lives.

Particular landscapes are associated with each of these activities. The family normally has a place called "home." In fact, social disruption is often associated with those environments that do not adequately provide for personal and family space—for homescapes. Economic landscapes can include everything from rural farms to urban industrial parks. Projections that many people will one day be employed in home environments supported by sophisticated communication systems raise as yet unanswered questions concerning the possible future separation of workers from traditional economic landscapes.

There are other universal requirements and associated landscapes that assume varying degrees of importance. For instance, there is a need for organization to provide protection within a societal framework—political landscapes. There is also a need to transmit culture from generation to generation—institutional landscapes. And one cannot overlook the human desire to find universal meaning, often met in religious landscapes.

Thus, there are universal requirements that foster relationships between people and their environments. Virtually everyone moves about, has conceptions of space that are important to their experience, and must partake of some sort of landscape experience. As with all universals, each individual attaches different magnitudes of importance to interaction with landscape. Some seem particularly sensitive to their surroundings and are what Steele would call "place people," while others are almost oblivious to place (1981, 44). However, landscape is part of everyone's experience, even if its impact is frequently subconscious.

When we look on unfamiliar places we may be tempted to see landscape as a static presence. Yet, we know that our hometown landscape is constantly changing. Analyzing our own place, we realize that landscape constantly says a lot to us about ourselves and that that message varies through time. For instance, the development of a previously vacant lot may please or anger residents as well as reveal something about contemporary economic conditions to trained observers.

In reconstructing the concepts of landscape and culture, recent work in cultural geography has emphasized the fact that the landscape concept is itself a sophisticated cultural construction: a particular way of composing, structuring and giving meaning to an external world whose history has to be understood in relation to the material appropriation of land. (Cosgrove and Jackson 1987, 96)

The nature of this universal human-environment relationship is a topic of inherent intellectual interest. When this relationship is better understood, observers will not only know more about human experience but also possess increased potential to intervene in that relationship.

People and the Meaning of Landscape

There is a duality involved in understanding landscape meaning. Landscapes have their own individuality, but that distinctiveness is perceived in many different ways. We bring our own conscious awareness to each scene, and to understand landscape meaning one must appreciate how individuals approach landscape comprehension. Anne Buttimer, who has studied the lives of practicing geographers (1983), says that geographers bring a "prefiguration" to landscape analysis. Prefiguration is defined as "an intuitive grasp of how the world is. Such prefiguration, which I call 'choreographic awareness' can best be understood as a poetic rather than a calculative exercise; it seems to involve moral, aesthetic, and emotional commitments which are related to lived experience . . ." (12). The intuitive awareness that geographers bring to spatial phenomena may be because they are particularly sensitized to environment. However, there is no reason to suspect that basic mental processes of others are inherently different.

The family, that comforting and most intimate of all universal institutions of learning, provides most of us with our first landscape imagery. House, yard, and neighborhood are the landscapes of our early lives. Our innocent experience in these spaces stays with us forever. Many people are convinced that viewing ancestral homescapes can tell us much about our forebears and their lives, conveying messages they can no longer share with us. Kevin Lynch says:

> To live in the same surroundings that one recalls from earliest memories is a satisfaction denied to most Americans today. The

continuity of kin lacks a corresponding continuity of place. We are interested in a street on which our father may have lived as a boy; it helps to explain him to us and strengthen our own sense of identity. (1972, 61)

Thus, the meaning of landscape is inevitably meshed with our sense of personal identification.

It is notable how often scholars mention the socialization processes when discussing how places acquire meaning. It is not so much that the meaning of places is taught; rather, it is assimilated, and that most often within the family circle. W. Lloyd Warner discusses this process with regard to objects (landscapes) in his book about the symbolic life of Americans.

The articulation of meaning to an object by an individual depends on previous experience of the individual with the object itself or with signs of the object. If it is with signs of the object ordinarily he will learn from others and be trained by them to bestow their meaning to the sign and thus to the object. If it is directly with the object the meanings for others will be reinforced or modified by his own experiences and by the meanings of the signs they use for it. The basic core of meaning for most signs and objects is acquired in infancy, childhood, and adolescence. However, the meanings of signs and objects shift through the individual's and the society's existence. The meaning of the Cross in the years 33 and 1954 is different and its meaning to a child being confirmed something other than to a dying man. (1959, 467)

In the past decade we have learned much through research that has differentiated between concepts of space and place (Tuan 1977, Relph 1980). This distinction highlights the fact that space can have a very impersonal dimension. That is, space as distance or area may simply be conceived of in some neutral or coldly quantitative fashion. On the other hand, place requires human significance linked to a particular location through individual or group experience and perception. The point is not to make some kind of artificial distinction between categories of locations, but to sensitize us to aurae associated with human experience in space. These experiences can range from highly impersonal action in public domains, to symbiotic relationships in the place we call home. To learn more about landscape meanings Edward Relph tells us to practice environmental humility, to sense but not impose values on landscapes (1981). He also asserts that we are going to have a great deal of difficulty trying to understand place meaning in a scientific mode for "place and sense of place do not lend themselves to scientific analysis" (1980, pref.).

Landscape perception is found in individual consciousness, and individuals sensitive to a sense of place in landscape find that human-environment interaction is a key ingredient in their lives. One can conceivably see landscape appreciation as a beneficial experience for everyone. However, there is potential bias in communicating landscape appreciation, for particularly sensitive individuals most often amplify landscape messages. It is entirely natural that some landscape observers are more sensitive than others. Yet, managing landscapes requires observant individuals to understand and interpret place meaning for more than a limited, hypersensitive audience. Comprehending widely held symbolic landscape messages makes us more sensitive to universal experience.

Landscape Messages

The beauty of the landscape portion of human-environment equations is that it tells so much about both parts. In fact, landscapes are much more expressive as visually observable phenomena than people are. We probably can't tell much about their home environments by observing people in neutral surroundings. However, landscape reading reveals a great deal about people who live, work, and visit that place. Our frequent first question to those we have just met—"Where do you come from?"—attests to our belief that place tells much about people.

When attempting to read landscapes it is worthwhile to remember that they are not quiescent. Landscapes have a message for us all. Kevin Lynch writes: "Any inhabited landscape is a medium of communication" (1976, 30). Lewandowski notes further: "As a system of nonverbal communication, the built environment must be decoded by those who use or observe it" (1984, 237). In other words, there is a demand on all of us to interpret our surroundings. Wagner calls landscape communication a dialectical process (1974). Thus, interacting with landscape is not an attempt to fathom a passive environment. Rather, it is participating in a dynamic give-and-take, problem-solving, human-environment relationship.

Landscape communication is effortless for most people. It is a natural act that occurs from our earliest days. However, those who would attempt to understand the broader spectrum of this communication must look deeply into human-environment relationships. Landscape messages come at many different scales—from places of national recognition such as the Washington skyline and from humble, personal landscapes. Understanding landscape meaning is similar to mastering a foreign language. We are all interpreters of landscape messages, but some have more facility and experience than others.

Experienced landscape interpreters begin by looking for different sources of symbolization. For instance, J. B. Jackson makes a distinction between vernacular and political landscapes (1984). Jackson's vernacular landscape is a creation of local custom, practical responses to circumstance, and everyday, unpredictable workings of society. The political landscape, on the other hand, is a result of planned action that imposes a certain kind of order on space. These two Jacksonian landscapes can, and in many places do, overlap. Edward Gibson detects a difference between elite and common understandings of the same landscape (1978). Different groups impose their interpretations on similar landscapes. A manicured park may represent order and stability to the middle class and repression to the poor. James Duncan studied symbolic landscapes in Sri Lanka (1985). He suggests that elites may try to associate themselves with powerful landscape messages in order to enhance or preserve their power. Commonly recognized landscape symbolization may be an ameliorating influence. Lester Rowntree and Margerit Conkey saw that preservation of the old city of Salzburg, Austria, lessened social stress through perpetuation of certain shared landscape symbols (1980). James Blaut notes that public understanding of common landscapes can come as a reaction to national trauma (1984). In his case the landscapes of human dimensions helped him come to grips with challenges to national identity posed by Vietnam, civil rights, and urban decay.

Politics in the United States is brimming with attempts to use landscape messages. Politicians routinely place themselves in certain settings in order to be associated with that landscape's message. Lyndon Johnson appeared at military bases to show how he supported a strong national defense. John Kennedy traveled to Appalachia to indicate concern for the poverty stricken. Ronald Reagan was pictured clearing his ranch land with axe in hand, sharing weekend chores with the masses. In other words, landscapes do a lot of political image-making.

Landscape messages can be conveyed by artifacts on the land, the material culture of a place. People of the distant past no longer talk to us, but remnant landscapes reveal more of their culture than they might be willing to share, even if they could. Buildings, fields, routes, gardens, and other landscape patterns speak of families, work habits, travel, tastes, and social structure. Landscapes explain life in the past and help us understand the ideas of another time and place (Glassie 1975). The challenge, of course, is to see, read, hear, or otherwise correctly sense landscape messages. This is not an easy task, as Tom Schlereth makes plain; "The language of any landscape is so dense with evidence and so complex and cryptic at times that we can never be certain we have read it all or that we have read it all right" (1980, 184).

Landscapes reflect societal conditions and shared messages. Familiar landscapes in the United States speak to our national identity. David Lowenthal notes that many historic sites have been preserved all over the country to convey the message of American liberties (1966). Citizens fear destruction of special places. National reaction to the farm crisis can be attributed in part to Americans' concern that rural virtues, expressed in pastoral scenes, may be declining along with the family farm (Lamme 1986). Agricultural change is natural. Yet, decaying barns and abandoned farms worry many Americans.

Perspectives on Innate Human-Environment Relationships

There is a class of studies that views people-place relationships as innately interactive, to be studied through methodologies linking the natural and social sciences. These studies contend that human landscape behavior is related to fundamental human needs. Jay Appleton's *The Experience of Landscape* suggests that people have an inherent need for certain types of environmental experience (1975). To Appleton, all animals, including humans, need to find protection as well as perspective in landscape. Thus, Appleton contends that places that provide security and unobstructed views are pleasurable for psychological reasons.

Any kind of a physiological connection between people and environment is bound to be controversial and hard to test (Craik 1986). Yet, most people have experienced repeated positive or negative reactions to certain landscapes. Highway beautification in the United States is an attempt to make traveling a more pleasurable experience by removing landscape elements that offend many people. Junkyards and excessive or oversized highway billboards are generally considered offensive, while pastoral views are thought to have a positive impact on our travel experiences. J. B. Jackson points out that human beings have a need to establish an emotional relationship with landscapes (1980, 18). We are not passive observers of environments. One of the reasons that familiar scenes are highly valued is that personal experiences are associated with those places. A logical extension of this idea is that different people with different backgrounds and different personalities have widely varying experiences in similar landscapes. Thus, a landscape that seems familiar and pleasant to one may go unnoticed or seem threatening to another.

A scholarly discipline that is related to the biological and psychological implications of landscapes is the field of perception. Perception is concerned with the mental ordering of environmental images. A host of factors influences the ordering of landscape images, among them landscape characteristics, the operation of the senses, the cultural attributes brought to landscape experience, and perhaps the evolution and functions of various portions of the brain. Saarinen reviews relevant fields concerned with these different areas of interest (1976). He points to the tremendous difficulties posed by attempts to integrate theories in these diverse fields, not the least of which is concern with measurement.

While appreciating perspectives on innate human-environment relationships, voluminous literatures and methodological pitfalls associated with these endeavors seem daunting.

> Thus, we confront the central problem: any landscape is composed not only of what lies before our eyes but also what lies within our heads. . . . Recognition of that fact brings us to the brink of some formidably complex matters. But it is not necessary to plunge into the technical thickets of optics, psychology, epistemology, or culture to converse intelligently about the topic. It's far too fascinating and important to be left fragmented and obscured in the jargon of such specialists. It deserves the broad attention that only ordinary language allows. (Meinig 1979, 34)

Behavioral and Contemplative Analyses

Systematic study of landscape requires clearly stated and consistently used methods of analysis. It would be helpful if there were an accepted paradigm ready for adoption with any study. However, this is not the case with landscape scholarship. A range of methodologies can be employed in landscape studies. In a superficial way it would seem that there are two fundamental and different approaches to human-environment analysis. For the purposes of this discussion the two categories are labeled behavioral and contemplative. These two categories are not, in fact, mutually exclusive. However, their differences provide a useful starting point for methodological discussions.

Behavioral approaches to human-environment studies in geography are direct descendants of positivist philosophy. As behavioral approaches were practiced during the sixties and later, they involved a strong emphasis on empirical research, scientific methodology, model building, and quantitative techniques. Behavioral research of that type has given way to a more subjective analysis of the processes involved in spatial behavior (Golledge and Couclelis 1984). The recognition that a non-empirical approach is important and the understanding that all science is value laden have altered behavioral research. While behavioral research dealing with human-environment relations is no longer strictly positivistic, it retains some earlier characteristics. These include an emphasis on theory and quantification.

Although behavioral geography has been suggested as a unifying concept for all environmental perception research, to date it remains most closely identified with attempts to apply rigorous scientific analyses to human spatial actions. There are strengths and weaknesses to this approach. On the positive side is the continuous development and application of appropriate quantitative techniques for available spatial data. Such data, in spite of their limited representation of reality, need to be taken into consideration. The negative side of behavioral approaches involves their frequent lack of sensitivity toward the extremely complex equation of human-environment relations. Assumptions built into behavioral models are often non-verifiable, rendering the whole exercise questionable. Nevertheless, it must be acknowledged that behavioral research on topics like cognitive mapping, place preference, and migration has raised interesting questions, even when failing to supply complete answers.

One of the strengths of a behavioral approach is its ability to predict. Research that models behavior in space makes it easier to speculate on future behavior (Rushton 1984). Thus, a challenge for other approaches is to formulate generalizations concerning behavior in space. It is possible that models derived from contemplative approaches, although less quantifiable, are more penetrating in determining true human experience and therefore can be useful predictors of the future. There are many statements contrasting what some have come to call scientific and humanistic approaches to geography. However, separation of these two approaches may be a false dichotomy. The scientific method, insofar as it aims to produce generalizations about human behavior in space, is found at least implicitly in all areas of geography.

A discussion contrasting the two approaches is found in John Leighly's presidential address to the Association of American Geographers (1958). Leighly's speech, delivered at a time when quantitative analysis was building momentum, contains an appraisal of naturalist John Muir's image of the West. After a review of Muir's work, which he labels "a Sierra of the spirit," Leighly discusses a growing dichotomy in geography between the scientific and the humanistic. He thinks of differing methods of geographic research as a spectrum of approaches. Leighly acknowledges that there is value to be found in all methodologies and suggests that more contemplative, humanistic approaches should not be forgotten in a rush toward pure science. He concludes, "we can still learn from him [Muir]: not only

about the West but also about the world in general and the joy
and wisdom that come from the contemplation of it" (318).

There is a point in our study of landscape when it becomes
necessary to join the scene—to merge with environments in
order to understand them. Looking in from the outside no
longer suffices. David Ley refers to this situation when he fore-
sees the need for "methodologies that enable the researcher to
understand and interpret the subjective-meaning contexts of
individuals and groups in their own milieu, in as non-obtrusive
a manner as possible" (Ley 1981, 217). In order to understand
action in the environment one often has to be a part of the
action.

Landscape observers are components of the scene they
observe. Many strive to understand place, and then, most
importantly, to communicate place meaning. Perspicacious
communication is vital to generate support for landscape
preservation. We naturally turn to the humanities for landscape writing exemplars. One of the finest landscape thinkers
and managers was the English poet Alexander Pope, who designed a number of eighteenth-century landscape gardens.
Peter Martin gives us a description of Pope's attitude toward
landscape (1984). In this passage, Martin is exploring the challenges Pope faced when writing about a particular place to a
friend.

> In order to describe enthusiastically a garden scene to Martha
> Blount, Pope had to feel that the place could offer her a sanctuary
> and mode of symbolic well-being, whether it was a wilderness like
> Netly Abbey or well-tempered garden like Sherborne. To put it an-
> other way, there had to be a feeling of Windsor Forest about the
> landscape, a sense of place that recalled that original landscape of
> affection and meaning in their lives, and evoked a setting where
> Pope could imagine her presence or "idea" as he put it. (212–13)

Martin's analysis is formulated in the language of the literary critic and not of the social scientist. His writing suggests a
depth of landscape feeling on the part of writer and subject.

Would that most landscape preservationists could communicate in this way. I love the phrase "genius of place," often used by humanists to describe a holistic conception of particular locations. This concept of landscape is a universal experience, not just appreciated by scholars. A sense of place is so difficult to grasp through sterile scientific analyses and writing.

Thus, a challenge for those working on the contemplative side of landscape research is to present an approach that is sensitive to place but not so idiosyncratic that it becomes usable only for particular observers (Bolton, 1987). Scholars must blend source materials and methods appropriate for places under evaluation. Methodologies may range from the scientific to the utterly contemplative. Most landscape research will utilize approaches drawn from both traditions. The unifying, consistent element is landscape itself and the questions asked about it.

If landscape interpretation and management could become a focus of geographical studies, a full range of human geographic methodologies would be directed toward a single problem area. The most tightly constructed research of behavioral geographers and the subjective interpretations of cultural geographers can be utilized in tandem for maximum effect. Methodological purity is a forgotten issue amid the excitement of landscape intepretation and what it reveals about the shared spatial experiences of mankind.

3. Landscape and Community Power

Cross Creek is a rural hamlet in North Central Florida. It is well known as the former home of Marjorie Kinnan Rawlings, Pulitzer Prize–winning author of *The Yearling*. Rawlings wrote a book about her adopted village that was made into a popular movie, *Cross Creek*, in the early 1980s.

Cross Creek is also a very special natural setting. The creek that gives its name to the village runs between two large lakes. Land in between these lakes is low lying with marshy shores, plentiful vegetation, numerous eagle nests, and a few remnant citrus groves. Early in this century citrus agriculture had retained a foothold in this relatively cold North Florida location because of the lakes' moderating effect on temperature.

These cultural and physical characteristics have turned Cross Creek into a popular recreational destination. The Rawlings home, now a state historic site, has attracted increasing numbers of visitors since release of the movie. Anglers and North Florida residents seeking weekend retreats come to fish and relax. Cross Creek is not a pristine landscape of immaculate homes with manicured lawns. It is an authentic middle-class recreational landscape with cottages, mobile homes, fish camps, and mom-and-pop stores.

Cross Creek's popularity has attracted attention from those seeking investment opportunities. Assuming that visitor counts continue to increase, there is potential return from investment in tourist facilities such as modern motels and restaurants. In addition, the amount of undeveloped land in the area is attractive to builders of homes and cottages. A key concern for people interested in natural and cultural conservation at Cross Creek has been whether appropriate safeguards are in place to cope with development pressure?

Cross Creek is classified as a "rural cluster" under the Alachua County Comprehensive Land Use Plan. Although it is only one of seventeen such places in the county, its attraction to preservationists and investors stimulated attempts to change land-use regulations for that community. Building density in the county is normally regulated from two structures per acre near cluster centers to one per twenty acres on agricultural land outside settlements. Opposing groups favoring widely divergent approaches to Cross Creek development suggested modification of these densities. Consequently, a special amendment to the Alachua County Comprehensive Plan was adopted in 1985 eliminating high-density tourist facility or housing development potential at Cross Creek. A novel feature of that amendment was a transfer-of-development-rights provision for those who lost development potential at the creek. In spite of this provision, the scene was set for a classic struggle between "developers" and "environmentalists" (Kinser 1987).

In response to these new land-use regulations a challenging legal suit was filed by eighteen Cross Creek land owners. Of a total 3,138 acres in the Cross Creek planning area, the plantiffs own approximately 1,300 acres. A large portion of their acreage is in undeveloped lakefront locations. These owners claimed that the Plan is a confiscation of property rights and that it was adopted in an illegal manner. At a May 1988 trial the presiding judge ruled that the plaintiffs failed to prove their case primarily because property had been sold profitably since adoption of the Plan. His dismissal of the suit is being appealed to a higher court.

Although the case is still before the courts and unresolved, it brings up two interesting and related points. First, several land owners as well as county planning officials expressed satisfaction at the prospect of a legal resolution of the case. Thus, both sides felt they were acting on principle and were willing to submit their stands to judicial processes. Second, among numerous local editorials dealing with this case, the opinion of a local business newspaper that normally represents development interests proved particularly interesting (McGurn 1988). The writer suggested that although developers recognize there are legitimate public rights to the preservation of special places, they feel these collective rights should not infringe on landowners' rights to be adequately compensated for their properties.

I take these observations as points of departure for a theory concerning landscape preservation—that *power over American landscapes is most effectively exercised in the context of Constitutional principles.* As a constant observer and sometime participant in land-use regulation cases, I have noticed a behavioral pattern among participants. There is frequent appeal by opposing groups to what I would call a landscape belief system based on "Constitutional" principles. In the case of Cross Creek this belief system was expressed in the participants' (1) willingness to submit to judicial processes in the belief that the right would prevail, (2) concern with property rights, and (3) recognition of the rights of the general public to a high-quality environment.

What is the Constitutional basis for these beliefs? The first two are based on the fifth amendment to the Constitution: "No person shall be . . . deprived of life, liberty or property, without due process of law; nor shall private property be taken for public use without just compensation." The third belief—that the public has a right to a high-quality environment—is more general in nature and comes from the Preamble to the Constitution: "We, the people of the United States, in order to . . . promote the general welfare. . . ." There are, of course, many things necessary for the general welfare, including preservation of historic landscapes as an important element of America's heritage (Lamme 1989).

People seem to feel better believing that their arguments are based on higher principles, understanding that principles can be in conflict, and having a reasonable degree of confidence in democratic paths toward equitable solutions. Some feel that people become less reasonable when dealing with conflicting principles. For instance, religious conflicts represent such strongly held beliefs that they often seem insoluble. In general, conflicts pitting property rights against common welfare rights are not as strongly held as conflicting religious, moral, or political beliefs. While it is not unknown for people to violently defend their property, such confrontations are unusual in the case of historic landscapes.

Why bother mixing an analysis of landscapes with a study of power in society? Because I am convinced that it is possible and profitable to interpret landscape change in a systematic way. Each landscape may be different, but a recurrent pattern of power strongly influences landscape evolution. To investigate my thesis I am forced to turn to disciplines other than my own. Experience has suggested that it is wise to tread lightly in other's fields of specialization, and I make no claim that my interpretation is of any relevance to their work. What I am really doing is shamelessly borrowing ideas that seem to be relevant to my own concerns. At the least, I hope to stimulate innovative thinking about power over landscapes.

Power and Historic Landscapes

Historic and common landscapes share many characteristics. However, preservation planning highlights differences between these two types of landscapes, for historic landscape management must respond to more people through more intricate institutional frameworks. Historic landscapes have powerful friends and foes.

The notion that a privileged elite has disproportionate control over many aspects of American life is not a new one. This is certainly the case with landscape control. "Most power resides with small groups or elites. These groups make choices which affect the history and future of particular landscapes" (Penning-Rowsell 1986, 123). There are those who argue that even the concept of landscape is an elite one (Cosgrove 1984). According to this view landscape concerns developed in feudal Europe among the landed gentry and remained a focus of upper-class value systems in the shift of wealth from land to capital. W. Lloyd Warner suggests that the upper classes have a natural affinity for certain types of landscapes that symbolize their values. Here he speaks of the pastoral elements preferred by the rich in urban settings.

> The beauty of the tree-lined street and the common sentiment of its residents for the venerable elms unify the homes of Hill Street in the minds of its people, the fine old trees providing an outward symbol of that superior region's self-regard. The trees themselves are part of a planting that physically and symbolically interrelates the contemporary families and their homes with the larger cultured world of their dwelling area, and their whole world with the values and beliefs of an upper-class style of life through past generations. In the living presence of the elms, the past lives too. (1959, 44)

The rich have resources to promote certain landscape values. Who else can afford space in an urban setting for extensive lawns, gardens, etc.? If a group or individuals feel strongly about landscape management and have resources to back up those feelings, landscapes are likely to mirror their wishes to some extent. In some cases environmental regulations that have been established through political processes reflect the tastes of the well-to-do. For example, the work of the Duncans has shown that elites effectively control the appearance of suburban landscapes through political action, the influencing of public opinion, the promotion of favorable land-use regulation, and by means of personal networks (1984, 237).

But there is more to this story. In spite of a seeming plethora of evidence supporting theories of a landscape conspiracy by the wealthy, landscape development is certainly not just the rich getting their own way. Every community has experienced cases where elite interests have been thwarted by opposition from other community segments. Landscape control is more than economic determinism. In the United States absolute individual or group power over anything is frowned upon. I believe that *control of landscapes is based as much on powerful ideas as on powerful people.*

Any study of landscape evolution profits from delving into the issue of who or what is controlling change. In our society this is a complex study, for sources of power are often obscure. Yet, management decisions concerning historic landscapes tend to be made in an arena that is at least partially political. Even where individuals or corporations decide to modify environments, such action typically requires governmental approval. Thus, in trying to determine who controls historic landscapes, one is drawn to investigate theories of political power.

Community Power

Power is the capacity to influence. The analysis of this capacity among groups of people is called the study of community power, and those involved in this study are drawn mostly from the ranks of political science and sociology. Although community power specialists have found inspiration in some sociological studies of American communities from the 1920s onward, the field developed critical intellectual mass during the 1960s. In fact, a paradigmatic contest that originated during that period still dominates community power literature. This contest is between advocates of the theories and associated methodologies of elitism and those of pluralism.

It would be misleading to assume that popular usage of those terms is indicative of theoretical position. Both theories have developed extensive and complex literatures, and arguments over terminology and interpretation have been carried to the limit. Those of us interested in power over landscapes should note two generally accepted assumptions: (1) communities are run by a relatively small group of leaders and not by the mass of the people; and (2) leaders exercise power within ideological frameworks that are directly related to landscape concerns.

Elite theory traces its beginnings to turn-of-the-century European writings (Bachrach 1967). At that time elite theory was often put forth as a justification for rule by an aristocracy. In America, elite theorists have been drawn from those critical of or desiring to reform the prevailing democratic system (Hawley and Wirt 1974, 4). Elite theory has been applied with considerable success to the understanding of government at the national level (Mills 1956). There an overlapping governmental, military, economic, and social leadership group dominates decision-making. Elite scholars suggest that this same sort of leadership structure exists at local levels.

Seminal work applying elite theory to a study of government at the local level was conducted by Floyd Hunter in Atlanta (1953). Hunter sought to identify and characterize people who were in positions of power. His method involved "reputational" research, surveying the reputed power of individuals in a number of ways. Hunter concluded that Atlanta is controlled by a small number of individuals with economic ties to one another. Thomas R. Dye, a leading elite scholar, states that a "consensus" is the key link betwen elites (1986, 33). Elite leaders are not members of some sort of conspiracy. Rather, they hold shared beliefs that lead them to act in similar ways, often in consort. Dye identifies elements of the consensus as belief in individual liberty, private property, and limited government (1981, 7). If elite theory was once the apologist for a class-conscious society, its current belief in a consensus hardly suggests radical departure from classical theories of democracy.

Although pluralism cites historical antecedents as well, its modern formulation and methodology can be viewed as a reaction to elite theory. As with elite theory, the seminal work for pluralists was an individual case study, in this instance, research by Robert Dahl on the community of New Haven, Connecticut (1961). Instead of surveying reputations of individuals in leadership positions, Dahl studied how particularly important issues were resolved. Issues chosen included public education, urban redevelopment, and political party leadership. His study of issue resolution enabled Dahl to identify influential individuals. He concluded that there was not much overlap in New Haven from leadership on one issue to leadership on another. Dahl's pluralist model of leadership allows for the possibility of change in membership and ideas. Thus, pluralist theory pictures a society divided into groups of people represented by leaders with different economic, labor, social, and governmental interests. These groups compete for power over particular issues. Electoral processes provide for leadership accountability to the interests of the groups.

Beliefs associated by some with pluralist theory are called a "democratic creed." This creed is composed of beliefs in political rights, such as the vote, free speech, petition, etc. (Waste 1987, 17). It should be emphasized that these beliefs are not as important to pluralists as the consensus is to elitists, for pluralist models stress the importance of competition among groups in contrast to elite theory's emphasis on a cooperation based on belief. Pluralists seem to be more satisfied with current systems of local power. That doesn't mean that they feel no improvements are necessary, only that they are confident they can be carried out within current power structures.

Because these two theories are focal points of a long debate, I have emphasized their differences rather than their similarities. Yet, both elitism and pluralism have acquired many qualifying adjectives such as "democratic elitism" and "privatized pluralism." As community power scholars expand their studies to more localities it becomes obvious that there is a spectrum of power structures. The spectrum ranges from places tightly controlled by a small number of individuals to those with highly segmented leadership within an open system (Trounstine and Christensen 1982, 40). Hawley and Wirt allude to what I call a spectrum when they say that ". . . distinctions between elite and pluralist systems are matters of degree rather than of mutually exclusive contrasts" (1974, 4). Prominent elite scholar G. William Domhoff writes: "If you take a look at the chapter on local power in my 1967 book, *Who Rules America?*, you will see that it is a brief and perfunctory effort that concedes the local level, at least in New Haven and a few other places, to the kind of pluralistic power conflicts that Dahl portrayed" (1986, 54). Dye and Ziegler make further concessions to pluralists:

> Thus, although descriptions of the power structures in American communities may differ only because social scientists differ in theory and methods of research, it is more likely that community power structures in the United States in fact range from monolithic elites to very dispersed pluralistic elites. (1981, 450)

So if community power scholars simply come to the conclusion that there are a range of community leadership systems, of what use is this literature to one interested in power over landscapes? Its utility lies in the fact that belief systems associated with both theories are crucial to landscape concerns. The consensus for elites is belief in individual liberty, private property, and limited government. Compare that with a suggestion by pluralist Robert Dahl concerning needs in future community power research:

> The third feature, which . . . I touched on in *Who Governs?* but which needs to be built on more extensively . . . is the effect of the belief system. This would involve a range of beliefs that would include the democratic creed, whatever that may be, but also other kinds of beliefs about the legitimacy of capitalism, private enterprise, property, and other beliefs that limit what municipal governments and local politicians can do. (1986, 192–93)

Similar belief system characteristics associated with the two theories are striking, even if such beliefs occupy a more strategic position in elitist theory. All these beliefs have a foundation in the United States Constitution.

I think that all these principles are relevant to landscape issues. However, concern for private property is clearly a fulcrum for power over landscapes. Elitists address private property beliefs in greater detail than do pluralists. Elitists contend that business interests built on a base of real estate investment are at the center of local power. Domhoff calls this local elite a "growth machine" and writes: "Although the growth machine is based on land ownership, it includes all those interests that profit from the intensification of land use, including developers, contractors, mortgage bankers and related real estate businesses" (1986, 59). Dye explains the logic of the growth machine. "Community elites strive for consensus. They believe that community economic growth—increased capital investment, more jobs, and improved business conditions—benefit the entire community" (1986, 33). Pluralists' recognition of the primacy of property interests in local belief systems is indicated by their selection of urban redevelopment as a key research issue. Robert Waste defends use of this issue because of its broad importance to many groups within a metropolitan area (1987, 80). In summary, elitists and pluralists recognize, in different degrees, the importance of belief systems in community power and the pivotal role of the principle of private property within those systems.

I believe that a widespread belief in individual and collective property rights as guaranteed in the Constitution is the foundation for power over landscapes. A vast majority of people on both sides of controversial issues will readily recognize, perhaps not dispassionately, the relevance of belief systems to problems at hand. Continually reminding those concerned with landscape planning of this Constitutional basis for notions of power over landscapes will increase the probabilities of achieving successful landscape preservation.

Beliefs and Behavior

A Constitutional belief system concept applied to landscape concerns through the actions of leaders can be thought of diagrammatically as two similarly aligned and interacting triangles. At the apex of a conceptual triangle are specifically enunciated Constitutional provisions concerning property, the role of government, and rights of individuals. Land-use regulation is directly related to these pillars of our society, pillars so universally recognized that they are frequently addressed in any debate concerning a specific landscape, as in "Zoning eliminates my property rights," "We have a right to vote on this annexation," or "The city is obligated to provide more open space," etc. As the conceptual triangle expands downward it encompasses laws, regulations, and procedures governing landscapes that have developed over a period of years and at many places through trial and error. It is at this level that debate focuses on ecological, commercial, educational, cultural and recreational issues, among others, surrounding particular landscapes.

This conceptual triangle is aligned with a leadership triangle with relatively few leaders having great authority at the top and increasing numbers of less influential people under them. Those at the top tend to pay more attention to overriding principles while those further down the triangle have to concern themselves with a broad span of practical matters. Successful landscape preservation today most often involves compromise between leaders and among competing principles. Compromise is supported by the belief system which balances competing, legitimate interests within an implicit Constitutional framework. Operationally the system promotes compromise among leaders seeking resolution of local issues in much the same manner as a laboratory experiment is deductively solved on the basis of an overarching law. It is unlikely that successful compromise can be initiated outside that framework.

I do not mean to suggest that only leaders influence landscape preservation. National Trust for Historic Preservation membership was approximately 200,000 in 1987, a membership that represents a cross section of American society. In addition, the public generally supports landscape preservation as part of sound ecological policy. In some instances mass input is sought through planning boards, hearings, and votes on particular issues. Grassroots support for preservation of all types is reciprocated by local, regional, and national leaders. A landscape preservation theory based on community power doesn't eliminate the possibility of public participation in preservation, but limits public influence to goals within the belief system. A broad-based compromise tends to be the most effective approach to any preservation goal. If landscape management is supported by public opinion, then the outlook improves for endangered landscapes. Conversely, little is accomplished in those places lacking a compromise on landscape issues.

Fortunately, leaders often embrace a landscape model that stresses preservation of natural and historic elements. Landscapes and, particularly, aesthetic appreciation of landscapes, is an ideal that has been especially appealing to the upper classes. Owning pastoral property is a notion as attractive to the well-to-do of today as it was in the past. Pastoral scenes seem to suggest a connection to the past, to imply a stable value system, and to establish the owner's credentials as a member of a traditional landed gentry. "Historical knowledge is by its nature consensual," says David Lowenthal (1985, 214). By this he means that a peoples' knowledge of the past goes through a production and verification process that ensures majority agreement. This belief in past acts and meanings is an important element in the appeal of historic landscapes. Exceptional landscapes are symbols of belief, not imposed, but accepted and recognized by large segments of society. As seemingly timeless elements of everyday life, historic landscapes symbolize national stability. They are at once personal property, historic relic, and national confirmation.

It is also true that historic landscapes are repositories of a "sense of place": widely recognized set of symbols and associations identified with a particular locality. Economist Roger Bolton has been trying to develop an economic interpretation for sense of place (1987). To Bolton sense of place is an intangible characteristic of a locality that makes that place attractive to people. Bolton's aim is to assess the value of this characteristic. To him, sense of place is an economic asset, and hence historic landscapes have investment requirements, require maintenance fees, and provide returns to investors. Personal or collective investment required to maintain landscapes, whether it be through ownership or political action, is repaid in the increased value of the property, its ability to attract paying visitors, its higher resale value, etc. Thus, an impulse to preserve historic landscapes can be based on emotional and economic return. These considerations are important enough to involve a broad cross section of society, and often leaders' recognition of the potential returns from landscape preservation enhances their willingness to make compromises.

It is important to remember that leaders are not just rich folks controlling everything but individuals from all levels of society who have risen to important decision-making positions through shared beliefs and achievement. Powerful people cannot do whatever they like with their land, for violation of a Constitutional landscape belief system through arbitrary, undemocratic process weakens leadership power. Active participation by professionals in elite decision-making processes exposes them to important landscape interpretations while providing opportunities to share expertise. Edward Gibson discusses working with leaders in the Vancouver area.

> When there is a public dispute about the future of a place, the evidence of meaning held by interest groups can be most easily collected. This may be done in a manner not unlike that of a good ethnographer engaged in the study of a culture beyond his or her own; that is, it is necessary to participate in the elites who coordinate, or speak on behalf of, their memberships. In order to form any

idea at all of the self-conscious or unself-conscious intentions of these elites, we are forced to be initiated into their structures and actively participate in meetings or even committee work. (1978, 153–54)

The professional in landscape evaluation and management consequently becomes a participant-observer in community power structures.

Just as community power analysts see a spectrum of power structures, preservation of any particular landscape may be achieved through elite or pluralistic approaches. The case studies in this book cover this range of possibilities. Elite, pluralist, or in between, preservationists are more likely to accomplish their goals when their attempt is based on shared Constitutional beliefs.

Preserving Landscapes

There is an arena of public action that frequently witnesses expressions of power over landscapes. That arena is the preservation movement. Preservation action can be a natural alliance between leaders and masses, since the public often supports preservation of those landscape elements that symbolize elite power. Estates, gardens, and open spaces have been elite domains in the past and are now preserved at public expense and with public agreement. More often, however, landscape preservation is controversial and contested.

Some theorists say we should take a hands-off approach to landscape, rather than maintaining or improving it. They argue instead for a greater appreciation of all landscapes (Relph 1984). Passive appreciation allows landscapes to develop "naturally" as environmental conditions change. An attraction of this passive approach is that it enables us to avoid making wrong decisions about what to change or preserve. For instance, commercial strips along urban arteries are roundly damned as eyesores. However, Grady Clay tells us that a commercial strip is a natural urban landscape. "The strip is trying to tell us something about ourselves; namely, that most Americans prefer convenience; are determined to simplify as much of the mechanical, service, and distribution side of life as possible; and are willing to patronize and subsidize any informal, geographic behavior setting that helps" (1973, 108). Clay's views seem to agree with those of J. B. Jackson, who criticizes preservation for its undiscriminating and uncomprehending approach (1984). The problem that Clay and Jackson point to is that preserving one structure or landscape excludes others. When preservation judgments are faulty, landscapes convey inappropriate messages.

David Lowenthal says that once we preserve a landscape, and identify it as being preserved, that place becomes less functional (1979, 111). Attempts to maintain functional landscapes while adding preservation controls foster a peculiar dilemma. Interrupting processes of landscape change makes landscapes less "natural." Lowenthal also says that the past is not preservable—what we work with is either "memory, history, or relics" of the past (1985, 187). The real past can never recur. John R. MacArthur, publisher of *Harpers*, doesn't like restoration of urban centers when it involves a pandering to popular image (1986). He points out that most urban cores of American cities were trade-motivated, with associated heavy industry and transportation. Establishment of boutiques in old warehouses is not really restoration, and it creates a false sense of history. MacArthur also challenges this sort of restoration as being economically unsound because it creates too many low-paying service sector jobs.

In spite of these legitimate reservations, it is unlikely that there will be a suspension of preservation efforts. Preservation, when it is done well, can be beneficial to wide segments and widely related interests within a society. Peirce Lewis contends there are a number of advantages to preservation, from the purely aesthetic returns through improved quality of life to economic gain (1975). Landscapes can be assets, and better-preserved landscapes are more valuable to society. In this context it should be remembered that good landscape preservation is not simply an attempt to recreate the past. Preservation should attempt to preserve essential sense-of-place elements within a changing societal framework: these are evolving historic landscapes.

If we agree that quality space around us—landscape—is important to society's well-being, then we are naturally led to a consideration of how to develop and maintain such places. To preserve might seem to be a fairly straightforward approach. However, when preserving landscape one is not dealing with physical objects that can be put away in a laboratory showcase. Preserving landscapes involves analyzing human spatial behavior and coping with behavioral changes. An initial hurdle faced by preservationists is to determine how people feel about landscape and, therefore, what should be preserved as essential sense-of-place characteristics. Scholarly research on environmental perception ought to be useful for those interested in preservation. Perception studies examine how people perceive their surroundings, and this understanding should lead to better planning. However, perception research has not been used by planners because its scholars frequently fail to present research results in easily understood, usable formats (Goodey and Gold 1987, 126–27).

Kenneth Olwig reviews attempts to develop and preserve Denmark's Jutland Heath (1984). He points out that contemporary ideas of what is "natural" are constantly changing. Some like a landscape totally untouched; others prefer agricultural landscapes; a few would like to allow development. Olwig concludes that landscapes represent a process, and preservation is regulating this process in relation to various scientific, historic, aesthetic, and recreational values.

Rural landscapes featuring unrestricted vistas are relatively easy to perceive as unified settings. Rural preservation is helped by this ease of perception. Urban townscapes with limited horizons often dominated by individual structures are harder to view holistically. As a result, urban preservation has concentrated on saving parts of townscapes. As one reviews the Register of Historic Places in the United States it quickly becomes apparent that urban structures are overrepresented, and there have been calls to rectify this condition in recent years (Lamme 1984). Urban preservation has achieved some satisfactory results. Old housing stock has been rehabilitated, bringing a better population mix to urban centers and strengthening the tax base. Consumers have been lured to downtown areas through creation of attractive shopping environments, often with historic overtones. Historic districts have helped to revitalize some neighborhoods.

Writing about urban preservation in Great Britain, M. R. G. Conzen addresses problems of maintaining holistic landscapes:

> Preservation has suffered from lack of funds, rigidity of application and exclusiveness of concentration on buildings to the neglect of town-plan features such as street spaces and their building lines and worst of all, preoccupation with isolated buildings of special merit as if an historical townscape were merely a lost assemblage of remarkable bits and pieces without spatial coherence or context. The geographical nature of historical townscapes as well as their role within the totality of planning claims on the land requires a more holistic approach. Instead of speaking merely of "preservation" it might be better to use the term landscape management as being less suggestive of restriction to physical preservation of practical and in a sense isolated landscape elements. (1981, 59)

For many people preservation means to emphasize historical landscape elements. Raymond Williams notes that people have a tendency to think of the past as preferable to the present and future (1973). Thus, in rural and urban settings we see attempts to blend contemporary usage with historic structural elements. Removal of neon signs, elimination of post–World War II building façades, highlighting building detail with exterior decoration, and labeling places in the "Ye Olde Watering Hole" tradition—all these create an impression of age and presumably elicit favorable reactions. That the public is attracted to old things and places is fortunate for historic landscapes. Places labeled historic can be marketed, and this is important in a capitalist society.

Many people would agree that the historic landscapes studied in this book are important and need to be "preserved." It cannot be said, however, that there is agreement on what preservation means and how it should be done. Despite its connotations of control and conspiracy, "management" is not a foul word for those interested in preservation. We cannot close our eyes to the fact that landscapes must and will be managed. We might as well, as professionals interested in preservation and utilization of historic landscapes, become participants in management processes.

A Hypothetical Example

Let's consider an example of how community power perspectives might help us understand and participate in historic landscape evolution. This hypothetical case should have a ring of truth, for it contains a plot played out in many communities.

Our fictitious place, Hometown, is a city of fifteen thousand located thirty miles from the capital and largest city of a Middle Atlantic state. Residents who enjoy a rural atmosphere commute to work in the capital. The local chamber of commerce hopes to attract high technology firms to an industrial park north of the city. A national park on the south side commemorates a historic site of national significance. The park includes one-third of fifteen hundred acres associated with the historic site. Roads leading to the park are lined by tourist service establishments and entertainment attractions.

A typical comprehensive plan calls for controlled development of all these activities. Policies and regulations would encourage housing construction for new residents at selected locations, industrial growth to increase the tax base, expansion of the national park to include much of the historic site, restriction on commercial strip development to certain roads, and maintenance of a small-town atmosphere.

While all this sounds reasonable, Hometown's plan has lots of critics. Old-time residents and environmentalists oppose new housing tracts; neighborhood associations don't want industrial development nearby; owners of land near the park support unrestricted development options for their land; and entrepreneurs catering to the tourist market seek locational flexibility for their businesses.

At first glance the application of the comprehensive plan described above would seem to involve denial of Constitutional guarantees of freedom. After all, such plans restrict individual liberty and property rights while increasing the powers of government. This superficial reaction is not accurate in a pragmatic world, for most people realize that land-use regulations are here to stay. A review of Hometown's plan from a Constitutional and community power perspective gives us an indication of its prospects for landscape preservation.

1. Successful planning is likely to be built upon a capacity to get support from a wide range of community leaders. Citizens have input, perhaps through direct votes, public hearings, and demonstrations, but over the long haul agreement among leaders is essential to success.

2. Leaders who must get behind the plan if it is to succeed already occupy positions of influence economically, politically, and socially.

3. Citizens concerned about a particular aspect of the plan may play important roles and move into leadership positions through accepted institutional frameworks. Thus, preservationists, businessmen, farmers, etc., have access to decision-making processes.

4. Leaders who influence adoption of the plan implicitly accept Constitutional landscape beliefs. In practical terms, this

means leaders must recognize that there are moderate limits on liberty and property rights, and moderate powers to be exercised by government. Individuals from extreme ends of the political spectrum, whether left or right, will have little influence in this process.

5. In the case of historic landscapes, the plan recognizes property interests of the nation as a whole. Those interests will tend to supersede, but not eliminate, the rights of local property owners and entrepreneurs.

6. There may well be a democratic struggle over elements of the plan between opposing groups in some political or legal forum. In community power terms, different leaders or groups may try to control the definition of the problem in an attempt to convince the public that one principle is more important than another. Most leaders and groups will be forced to accept landscape changes that are less than ideal. When a final compromise solution is reached, viewing these departures from a particular ideal in a context of Constitutional landscape beliefs will make them more palatable.

7. Once adopted, the plan will be administered by leadership representatives with little input from citizens. Changes in the plan are most likely to be incremental and at the behest of group interests.

Individuals, or even groups, who can singlehandedly preserve our landscape heritage are few and far between. Almost universal requirements for some type of planning create situations where leadership beliefs and compromise are essentials for landscape preservation. Planning requirements hinder landscape despots and make preservation more feasible. They also increase chances that nothing will be done, for, without belief-inspired compromise, preservation is unlikely to succeed.

Community power provides a perspective for the analysis of the evolution of specific historic landscapes in the past and prospects for the future. Evidence cited in the case study chapters suggests that strategies incorporating a Constitutional landscape belief system compromise are absolutely essential for the establishment of progressive landscape policies. This is not a prescription for preservation success, for competing plans may both be compatible with a Constitutional belief system. In such a case, dilution of leadership power would tend to militate against successful adoption of preservation action. Effective landscape preservation is most likely where a single plan within the belief system develops broad-based support.

Power over landscapes flows from Constitutional principles of property ownership, the common good, and democratic processes for conflict resolution. Community power perspectives enlarge our understanding of landscape evolution by identifying the various power structures and recognizing the role of belief systems. These perspectives also suggest which paths lead toward optimal landscape preservation. This study now moves to analyses of four different places and their history with regard to the development, management, and utilization of their historic landscapes.

4. St. Augustine, Florida

Eminent preservation historian Charles Hosmer identifies St. Augustine, Florida, as a site of significance to the preservation movement in the United States. In *Preservation Comes of Age* he writes: "It is possible to argue that this Florida resort community did take a leading position in the preservation movement for a while simply by providing a model" (1981, 322). This model for preservation featured a cooperative effort among leaders from all levels of government and private enterprise. However, this initial cooperation in St. Augustine failed to sustain itself, and thus, in spite of his kind comments, Hosmer's overall evaluation of St. Augustine preservation is not positive. A perusal of the St. Augustine scene by urban planners, cultural geographers, or preservationists must note the uneven results of a number of years of landscape management. This urban landscape contains sites whose authenticity and interpretation are thoroughly acceptable. However, the same landscape has advertised "historic attractions" possessing extremely doubtful credentials amid commercial clutter, and these detract from the overall experience.

Analyzing a site's particular sense of place is an essential task when one is considering landscape preservation. The past is present in landscapes, for "place character is the result of historical evolution, and thinking of how to conserve or enhance that character is illuminated by knowing how it came to be and what historic forces still sustain it" (Lynch 1976, 72). Thus, attempts to understand, evaluate, or prescribe for a historic place

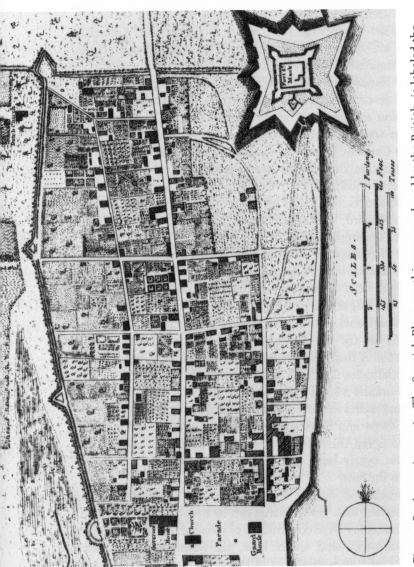

Fig. 1 St. Augustine, 1764. The Spanish Plaza, on this map produced by the British, is labeled the "Parade." Main streets run parallel to the Matanzas River shoreline, with houses set to the front of lots and gardens behind. The Castillo dominates the shoreline. Walls separate the city from nearby fields. (Original in Library of Congress)

a mixed racial—Spanish and Indian—town on the margin of Spain's colonial holdings. Local foodstuffs prepared in Indian styles and with local pottery were characteristic of the culture. A major landscape feature, during later years of Spanish occupation and ever since, is the Castillo de San Marcos located on the northeast edge of the town. A series of wooden fortifications had occupied this site and others nearby. The current Castillo, built of rock quarried on nearby Anastasia Island, was started in 1672 and completed just twenty years before the arrival of the British.

Most Spanish inhabitants and Indians were evacuated before the British took possession of Florida. Eventually these people were replaced by small numbers of Englishmen and some loyalists from colonies to the north. The English established commercial ventures in their provinces of East and West Florida and attempted to lure settlers to them. In St. Augustine, Englishmen took over former Spanish homes and extensively remodeled them. The so-called oldest house in St. Augustine was constructed during the English period on top of Spanish foundations. Florida was returned to the Spanish as a result of the English defeat in the American Revolution.

A final Spanish period from 1783 to 1821 was an interlude of little lasting importance. Few Spanish returned, and the former English provinces lapsed into a no-man's-land of lawless confusion. In the countryside Indians from Georgia and Americans from newly created states contended for open land. St. Augustine became even more of a backwater in the slowly diminishing Spanish Empire. A newly emergent and aggressive nation to the north would not long allow ineffective foreign control over the Florida peninsula. Florida was acquired from Spain in 1821 and became an American territory. Sparsely populated and settled only in the north, Florida occupied a marginal role in yet another nation's territory. Statehood, secession, and reconstruction occupied the rest of the nineteenth century. While these were important times for Floridians, events in

Florida could not have seemed very important to the rest of the nation.

From the middle nineteenth to the middle twentieth centuries ideas about Florida underwent significant change. This change, while not directly concerned with St. Augustine, would have a major impact on the city. The dominant image of Florida for the first three hundred years of its settlement was as a barrier to east-west travel. Jutting out from the continent in a southeasterly direction, the peninsula blocked shipping. The shortest route for sailing ships to get from the Caribbean to North Atlantic routes to Europe was through the Straits of Florida, between the Florida Keys and Cuba. This is a dangerous passage.

Perception of the peninsula primarily as a deterrent to shipping continued during the early American period. Southern Florida was relatively uninhabited and of little interest as a potential destination. Key West was a city only because of its location on the Straits. In the public mind Florida still stuck like a sore thumb into the Caribbean. Some way was needed to cross the peninsula. During territorial days there was widespread interest in proposals to accomplish this goal through waterways of various sorts and then through rail lines.

A reorientation of Florida's image to a north-south perspective came with arrival of a unique group of entrepreneurs in the last years of the nineteenth century. Men like Henry Flagler and Henry Plant saw Florida as a potential destination, rather than a barrier to be circumnavigated. To them Florida was a land of opportunity for those with investment ideas. Transportation improvement followed by land development started transforming Florida into a popular tourist destination known eventually as the "Sunshine State."

Meanwhile, St. Augustine had passed the years as a pleasant winter resort of modest size. Even though it was located at the northeast corner of the state, St. Augustine was very difficult to reach until the turn of the century. Travelers used coastal steamers or mixed-mode overland transport to reach the City.

Henry Flagler acquired his fortune working for the Standard Oil Company. He first visited St. Augustine seeking a healthful climate for his ailing wife. Flagler's business acumen told him that Florida in general, and St. Augustine in particular, had undeveloped potential as a holiday destination. Flagler started his Florida empire in St. Augustine in 1885. There he sponsored the creation of a new architectural style, Spanish Renaissance, and constructed a grand hotel, the Ponce de Leon. New tourist facilities and arrival of Flagler's railroad stimulated travel to the city and a modest increase in population. However, Flagler's vision was not confined to St. Augustine. Other entrepreneurs were developing southern parts of the peninsula, and he joined that effort. As his railroad and string of hotels extended further south, St. Augustine became a stop along the way to other places.

Historian Thomas Graham's description of St. Augustine's failure to become a tourist center identifies problems that persisted into the twentieth century.

> The continuing poverty of St. Augustine was one of the factors which ultimately prevented it from becoming the glittering winter resort of the nation Flagler has planned. That dull unprogressiveness which gave the town its quaint charm also made it discouragingly dingy and slow. The *Tatler* constantly scolded local merchants and town officials for their negligence in sprucing up the community to make it more attractive for the tourists, but few local men had the breadth of vision, and none had the resources, to aspire to the superlative heights Flagler sought. "Shall this be the Newport of the South, or Coney Island?" exploded the *Tatler*. But it was too late. (1978, 203)

This early recognition of a lack of vision among local leaders was prophetic for preservation opportunities missed in the future.

Thus, after the first quarter of the twentieth century St. Augustine was a city with a settlement history of approximately three hundred years. Its heritage was unmatched by any other urban area. Relatively large numbers of tourists passed through, some stopping for a visit. With historic resources to rival any city in the country, plus many visitors in the area, there was obvious potential for combining preservation and tourist development. This pleasant coincidence of economic development factors became apparent to a number of individuals who tried to manage historic landscapes in St. Augustine.

Factors Affecting Landscapes of St. Augustine

Every landscape is affected by many factors. Various people, such as founders, political leaders, business people, home owners, etc., influence the layout of places. Regulations including zoning codes, building codes, and environmental law control some changes. Unpredictable events in the past and present, like depressions, fires, and storms affect the look of the land. Many of these factors work independently and seemingly at random to produce the current scene. Landscape change is normally confined within a Constitutional landscape belief system, and in spite of numerous factors influencing a particular scene, it is often possible to isolate several that seem to be particularly influential at any particular place.

Individual Leaders
Translating general belief in Constitutional principles into action in support of historic landscapes is not easy. It calls for broad perspectives and, sometimes, denial of self-interest. These perspectives need to be articulated. Unfortunately, there is no generally accepted landscape ethic that would automatically prompt landscape preservation. Leadership action is mandated when responsibilities for decision-making are clear, as with a corporation, by law, or city charter. Where responsibilities are assigned, there is required decision-making. Yet, even here there is a range of effectiveness. For example, a decision can be made not to apply a rule or regulation. Making no de-

cision is a form of decision-making when it comes to historic landscapes.

City regulations require action with budgets, police and fire protection, education, etc., by specific officers and groups. Control of historic landscapes is seldom that clear cut. Zoning and planning regulations, if they mention landscape concerns, often address them in the most general policy terms, enjoining builders to "preserve neighborhood quality," or "be sensitive to historic resources," and so forth. Specific authority for control of landscapes is rarely granted. At parks or monuments controlled by governmental agencies, on the other hand, specific landscape authority is frequently assigned. An example of this is Castillo de San Marcos in St. Augustine. But, even in such cases, holistic landscape management may take a back seat to housekeeping matters.

When it comes to a city like St. Augustine, historic townscape leadership is not specifically delegated to any particular individual or group. Many people have had an influence on development of that historic townscape. Has a leadership compromise based on Constitutional principles evolved into an effective plan of action for St. Augustine's historic townscape? The townscape of today suggests the primacy of happenstance over such reasoned compromise. In spite of the apparent unplanned nature of historic townscapes in St. Augustine, there have been efforts to address effective preservation. Most St. Augustine officials have been concerned about their city's image in the eyes of casual visitors, and many individuals and groups have expressed an active interest in public interpretations of St. Augustine.

In preparing the manuscript of *Preservation Comes of Age*, Charles Hosmer conducted extensive interviews with many leading figures in the preservation movement. These people were active between the two World Wars, when preservation received its greatest impetus in this country. Hosmer's interviews are a major source of information on American preservation experiences. A number of these individuals had experience in St. Augustine. Through Hosmer's book and his oral histories we get a picture of the evolution of St. Augustine's townscape during that important period.

This must have been a time when hopes ran high for an improved preservation program in St. Augustine. In addition to increased commitment from Washington in the form of National Park Service control of the Castillo, the Depression and resulting expenditure of federal funds created more opportunities for St. Augustine to attract funding and people qualified to do work in historic development. Not to be ignored was the fact that a major restoration at Williamsburg had begun during the 1920s and that this sort of project was thought of as a desirable goal by many communities.

In 1933 a National Park Service superintendent arrived to take charge of the Castillo. Until that time, as with many historic military sites in the United States, the War Department had nominal control over the fort. The War Department had given local control to St. Augustine's historical society. The society in turn leased the fort for souvenir sales. The National Park Service had little sympathy with this approach to administration of a historic resource, and dispatched Herbert E. Kahler to St. Augustine to take charge. Kahler knew what he was supposed to do. "My job was to ease the fort away from those people as gently as I could" (Hosmer 1970 interview). Kahler quickly realized that there was more to the preservation problem in St. Augustine than getting a souvenir shop out of the Castillo.

Local people interested in developing historic resources of the city were divided. One active group was the St. Augustine Historical Society, which included many social elite. These old-line society members were not as directly tied to the tourist trade. Their motive was community pride, and they did not see eye to eye with politicians in the city. Another group was composed of businessmen whose base of power was the city council and Mayor Walter B. Fraser. Fraser owned the "Fountain of Youth Park," built around the legend of Ponce de Leon's supposed search (for which there is no accepted historical evidence). He was operating a tourist attraction which would hardly be compatible with standards of historic preservation. Yet, in his capacity as political leader, Fraser was instrumental in seeking support from preservation professionals.

Kahler was the first of a number of outside professionals to arrive on the scene, and he seems to have been the perfect person for the job. Hosmer describes him as "gentle, diplomatic, and easygoing" (Hosmer, 314). Besides recruiting a good staff, Kahler interested others in St. Augustine work. One of these was the director of the Carnegie Institution, John C. Merriam. To get a philanthropic foundation interested in St. Augustine was a major coup. Funding from private and federal sources outside the community would encourage citizens and ease pressure on local financial resources.

Although no one knew it at the time, the high-water mark of a joint effort to promote St. Augustine preservation came in October 1936. In Washington, at a meeting called by Fraser and Merriam, representatives of all interested parties sat down to plot St. Augustine's preservation program. As a guiding spirit of the group, and its temporary chairman, Merriam laid out a series of steps that should be taken preliminary to development of a comprehensive preservation plan. These included (1) compiling a comprehensive map and data about old St. Augustine, (2) surveying the degree of authenticity of the old section of town, (3) collecting maps of surrounding territory including aerial photographs to show changes through time, (4) collecting data on original flora and fauna, and (5) compiling documentary sources. Two committees were appointed. One was to proceed with collection of all information that was available on historic St. Augustine. A second committee was to develop guidelines for restoration and preservation. Meanwhile, the Carnegie Institution with help from the mayor's office set up a research program in the city. It was headed by a distinguished former director of historical research for the National Park Service, Verne Chatelain.

The committee reports published in March 1937 were the work of professionals. They pointed out that St. Augustine had gone through a number of stages of important historical development and was still a living city. In contrast Williamsburg, which was then in the beginning phase of restoration, had slept away the years on a relatively isolated peninsula in Virginia. St. Augustine, although not a hotbed of activity, had been on a major north-south transportation route and had developed into a minor tourist center. There was less authentic remnant townscape in the Florida city. Therefore, it was considered unwise to direct preservation toward any particular period.

Those interested in St. Augustine preservation had created a forum to discuss the directions preservation should take, but there was no resulting compromise on the subject. Mayor Fraser was mainly interested in restoration within the old city area. This would be restoration in the Williamsburg mold. Verne Chatelain and the Carnegie Institution had in mind an interpretive program that harmoniously integrated various historical facets of the city, without major emphasis on one period, and the reconstruction effort that would entail. The plan of the committee also called for effective zoning, building of recreational facilities and settings, and historic district controls. Kahler's review of the report for the director of the National Park Service emphasized the enormous amount of money and considerable time that would be needed for such a large-scale effort (1937).

The basic machinery was in place to involve a broad spectrum of individuals in St. Augustine preservation. Preservationists were highly motivated because the city was the major remaining Spanish colonial landscape in the East. The federal government was interested because of its ownership of the Castillo. Floridians throughout the state and locally were interested in developing historic resources and attracting tourists. However, local business leaders were not able to close ranks with national preservation professionals. For the next dozen years efforts continued to try to stimulate St. Augustine preservation. A number of factors hampered effective action. Among these were a change of leadership at Carnegie that cut off funding, lack of local and state supporting appropriations, and the advent of World War II.

St. Augustine preservation has always gotten mixed reviews. While the effort of the 1930s and 1940s cannot be called a failure, it was something less than a success. An unprecedented opportunity existed to bring leaders at many different levels together to affect change. But somehow the different images each group envisioned didn't mesh. There was no compromise based on Constitutional principles to support the preservation effort. It is often difficult for local leaders to reach total agreement on townscape development. The most successful sites are those where city planners have managed to reach a compromise that most leaders can support. Then appropriate controls, such as regulations and institutional guidelines, are put in place to carry out that compromise.

Contrast the situation in St. Augustine, for example, with the preservation efforts around the same period in Charleston, South Carolina, as described by Hosmer. "Charleston produced a remarkable generation of activists in the 1920s and 1930s whose interests and personalities seemed to balance one another. They were individualists who fought among themselves at times, but they always had a great common goal" (274). A "common goal" or compromise based on principles derived from the Constitution is what St. Augustine lacked. As a result, St. Augustine's townscape today represents a confused symbolic message of contradictory images.

Mixed Land Use

A "living city" presents special problems to people interested in management of historic landscapes. Such a place must make provision for many different functions that are necessary in any urban setting. The walled-off setting of a Williamsburg or a national park does not have to contend with this issue. At such places planners can concentrate on a primary preservation mission to the exclusion of others. But a city's primary mission is to be a central place that accommodates every urban function. The fact that St. Augustine is a functioning modern central place is both a weakness and strength from the historic townscape point of view. On the one hand, there will be continual pressures from diverse interest groups, and yet the setting has the advantage of being real—a non-artificial, evolving environment. The challenge is to try to maintain a historic sense of place within an active urban scene.

Mixed usage in any particular setting involves the emotional issue of control or in belief-system terms—limited government. In most cases it is not a question of no control versus total control. Rather, it is finding a happy medium that allows sufficient freedom to encourage individual enterprise while limiting those activities that would detract from the character of the place. St. Augustine has faced this problem for a long time. Exhibiting a typical old South antipathy toward land-use controls, leaders and residents resisted effective urban zoning until the 1950s. An exacerbating factor with a place like St. Augustine is that people who come to visit a prime historic site like the Castillo are targets of commercial activity. Merchants try to locate their activity as close to the fort as possible.

St. Augustine fits the classic American "tourist trap" mold. A letter to Merriam from a local historian during the period of the Carnegie Institution's first efforts in St. Augustine recited the concerns of those who were interested in authenticity of presentation. "St. Augustine is dominated by the exploiters of mercenary fakes based on falsifications of the city's history and operated for the hoaxing of tourists" (Hosmer, 316). Merriam commissioned a friend to visit the city and evaluate the prospects for preservation. Newton B. Drury, future director of the National Park Service reported on his impression of Fraser's Fountain of Youth Park. "As a study in human gullibility and an indication of what a large section of the public apparently wants, it was worth the price of admission which I did not pay" (1937).

During post–World War II years the president of Colonial Williamsburg, Kenneth Chorley, was asked by Walter Fraser to evaluate preservation potential at St. Augustine. Fraser, by then a state senator, had always hoped for a Williamsburg-type program. Chorley responded that Williamsburg restoration was not feasible in St. Augustine because of the relatively small number of authentic structures. In addition, he noted that there was a considerable problem with the reliability of various historical presentations (1947). Today the problem remains at St. Augustine to find a plan that can accommodate public usage, authentic historic presentation, and tasteful private enterprise. Private interests are entrenched in the historic district of St. Augustine, and no acceptable standard for commercial activity has been established to suit every entrepreneur.

One approach to the alleviation of this problem is through a State of Florida interpretive program called "San Agustin Antiguo." This program is active along St. George Street in the heart of the historic district. Some houses and gardens are interpreted by the state, that is, for a small fee tourists can visit these locations and see exhibits and demonstrations. A map for visitors pinpoints various historic locations. Interspersed among these places are structures listed on the map as being "under other auspices." Some of these places are churches and private homes. Others are run by purveyors of the "oldest" syndrome. The so-called Oldest Wooden Schoolhouse, Oldest Store Museum, etc., are private operations of dubious authenticity. Professionals and preservation purists tend to shake their heads at the mixed patterns of usage found in St. Augustine's historic townscape.

Evaluating Landscapes
Preserving and protecting landscapes sometimes requires taking a methodical approach to their evaluation. In establishing a system for evaluation of landscapes we can rely in part on work that has already been done in historic preservation. These methods of analysis are not so much readings of the landscape

as they are judgments of its historical significance. In fact, there are many checklists, some in great detail, contained within reports and ordinances dealing with historic preservation (Williams et al. 1983). For instance, a review of the Alexandria, Virginia, historic district ordinance that sets criteria for structural eligibility gives a good idea of major considerations involved in evaluations of historic significance (Murtagh and Argan 1983, 131).

1. Is a particular structure already listed on some type of historic registry?

2. Does the structure reflect the architectural, cultural, political, economic, societal, or military history of the nation, state or community?

3. Is the structure associated with people or events of national, state or local importance?

4. Is the structure a good example of architectural design, craftsmanship, or method of construction?

5. Is the structure the work of a recognized architect or builder?

6. Does the structure foster civic pride or enhance its attraction to visitors?

These same questions can be asked of landscapes. A particular landscape may be, variously, part of a historic district, representative of important historical movements or periods, associated with prominent people and events, outstanding in terms of design, and certainly an important element increasing attractiveness to visitors. If a historic landscape meets these standards it deserves the attention of preservationists.

Checklists of this sort are useful to determine if a structure or landscape is important enough to preserve. Such lists may prove helpful to initiate preservation action for historic landscapes of local significance. However, in most cases historic landscapes are already identified. These lists do not pinpoint key elements within a particular landscape that need to be preserved or changed. The need for this type of analysis is greatest with urban landscapes, where there is constant pressure to change.

M. R. G. Conzen, writing about conservation of British townscapes, suggests some landscape characteristics as worthy of the preservationist's concern (1981, 85–6). There should be concern with analysis of the holistic quality of the landscape, that is an overall impression that it gives the viewer or that it represents in cultural context—we might also call this its sense of place. Further, the impression should be evaluated in terms of how easy it is to understand, whether it represents enduring aesthetic values, and if it is accurate in terms of historical presentation. Conzen also suggests the scale of the townscape be taken into consideration—do structures and people mesh in visual harmony? Finally he would have us be aware of the need for adequate governmental control over historic townscapes. Datel and Dingemans list a few other qualities of historic landscapes that should be considered by preservationists, those of human scale, antique texture, harmonious architecture, mature landscaping, romantic associations, and traditional appearance (1984, 143). Many of these characteristics are identified subjectively and can be pinpointed for local leaders by landscape planners and consultants.

In all landscape evaluation it must be remembered that both places and people are the focus of attention. There is a reciprocal relationship, an exchange of symbolism (Ley 1981, 220). Landscape acquires meaning from human interpretation, and people acquire identity through association with place. "The proper study of landscapes may not be the landscapes themselves, but rather the people who experience them and the human feelings and meanings evoked by external surroundings" (Zube et al. 1975a, 3). Dealing directly with human reactions to place is not easy. Lynch has noted that when considering experience in space "there is not an organized theory for dealing with sensory data" (1976, 119). A number of approaches are possible. We can try to understand precise psychobiological reactions to place (see chapter 2). This is a controversial and untested area of landscape studies. We can also attempt to survey visitors (see chapter 7). However, such surveys are notoriously difficult to conduct, and the interpretation of results involves a high degree of subjectivity. Finally, we can look to our own experience in a place.

Is it possible that our individual experience of a place can be anything more than a personal, biographical account? Won't such an account simply be subjective musing that is worthless for social science? We, you and I, are the folk that experience historic landscapes. I believe that high-quality folk experience of our environment is an essential ingredient of "life, liberty, and the pursuit of happiness." This phrase from the Declaration of Independence is embedded in Constitutional definitions of liberty and is an important element in the kind of belief system that will stimulate public support for landscape preservation.

In addition to our own experience, using the experiences of those who are trained to interact with landscapes—be they planner, artist, writer, or preservationist—can also add a special dimension to landscape analysis. Ian Laurie has suggested that art critics are particularly well suited to analyze landscape qualities.

> This selection in no way implies an elitist view that only trained designers appreciate beauty, but simply that training develops skills of rationalizing judgment and a vocabulary of description and methodology of assessment, and it is therefore realistic to make use of this. Trained assessors do, of course, only act as the representatives of the society in which they work and which trains and establishes the judgements that (if the necessary democratic controls exist and are used) are subject to confirmation, modification, or rejection by society in making its decisions. Feeling and response to beauty itself is not, of course, necessarily the product of training or education, and its manifestation is seen in all sections of society. (1975, 106)

Experiments comparing landscape assessments of so called "expert" and non-expert groups have in fact shown a high degree of agreement on the basic aesthetic value of a site (Zube 1975b, 156).

Another reason for using evaluations of seasoned observers, however, is that these individuals are most likely to have skills necessary to communicate their findings. "The aesthetic arguments need to be presented precisely, if not quantitatively" (Cooke and Doornkamp 1974, 325). Regional novels, landscape paintings, and poems are effective because creative artists find creative ways to share feelings about place.

As a lover of landscapes I have attempted to understand my own reactions, often an immediate emotional response, to place. In trying to isolate the components of that response I have developed several evaluative instruments. These instruments are intended for use by expert observers. By expert I mean that they are not suitable for immediate use by the general public. At a minimum, some sort of training is required to standardize results. The individual scholar or professional office may find them useful. A number of other instruments of this sort are available for use by preservationists (Zube et al. 1975a). The utility of my instruments is limited; their main function is to help me identify elements of interest in particular landscapes. These instruments also assist in identification of problems at any place. Results obtained at different locations by untrained or dissimilarly trained observers would not be comparable.

A "Sense-of-Place Profile" is intended to highlight characteristics of a landscape that are most influential among observers (see Appendix A). The characteristics listed are divided according to whether they are innate qualities of the place or have to do with human activity. Computing a rating and significance score puts each characteristic in proper perspective in terms of overall evaluation. Irrelevant characteristics are not scored.

The "Compatibility Matrix" is designed to give observers an immediate indication of types of experience that visitors can expect at any place (see Appendix B). Categories of experience are those that are normally sought at historic landscapes.

Historic Landscapes of St. Augustine

Any interpretation of the townscape of St. Augustine must note that the symbolic message is complex and of varied quality. Since St. Augustine is an urban area, with high population density and mixed land use, the complexity of the message is not surprising. However, its variable quality and commercial tone is a result of years of failure to achieve a unified program of historical interpretation.

The historic district encompasses an area between the Castillo and the Plaza (Fig. 2). Here, along St. George Street, is the tourist hub of the city. Although other areas of the city attract some visitors, most public activities are in this section.

The Colonial Plaza
The town plan for St. Augustine was specified by the Law of the Indies (Crouch et al., 1982). These royal edicts established standard plans for colonial cities held by Spain. Thus, St. Augustine's is not special because of its originality of plan but because of its unique position as a Spanish colonial city in Florida.

The Plaza was the focus of colonial life for Spanish residents. Here the three authorities of Spanish policy were headquartered. The military, responsible for the maintenance of Spanish control often shared a structure on the Plaza with civil authorities. During the initial stages of settlement, military and civilian leaders might be the same. In addition, religious authority, that omnipresent companion of Spanish exploration, was found on the Plaza in the form of a church. At first this structure was humble, providing for spiritual needs of inhabit-

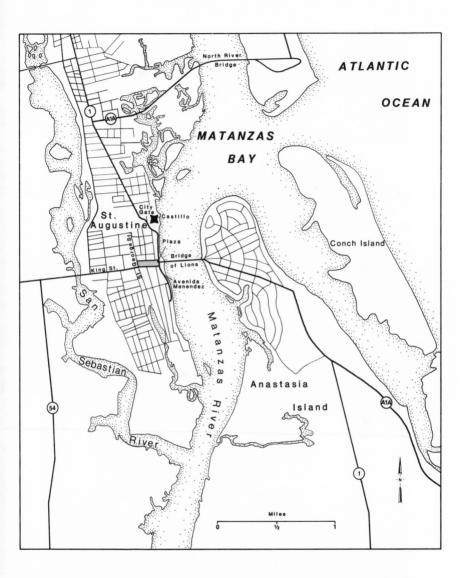

Fig. 2   St. Augustine, 1987 The Bridge of Lions connects Anastasia Island
to the Plaza. Coastal Route A1A turns north at the Plaza and passes between
the Castillo and the historic district. St. George Street, between the Plaza and
the Castillo, is the location of "San Agustin Antiguo," the Florida State
Interpretive Program. (Cartography Lab., Dept. of Geography, Univ. of Florida)

Fig. 3 The Plaza, St. Augustine. Traffic exiting the Bridge of Lions can go straight to the Plaza or turn right toward the Castillo. A high-rise bank building dominates the north side of the Plaza. The towers of Flagler's Ponce de Leon Hotel can be seen in the background. The center of the Plaza, now occupied by trees, buildings, and monuments, was open in Spanish colonial days. Today there is little reminiscent of colonial Spain about the Plaza. (Photo by author)

ants. However, as time went on church structures became more imposing. Large structures and enclosed grounds were better suited to handle many parishioners. In a place like St. Augustine, the church came to be called a cathedral and often was the headquarters for a bishop. Other structures on a plaza could include homes of the well-to-do and some commercial establishments. Plazas were literally and figuratively the centers of Spanish colonial cities.

Time has not dealt well with St. Augustine's Plaza (Fig. 3). Being a node of central-place activity, the Plaza has been subjected to urban pressures without a corresponding sensitivity to its past. For a number of years, the Plaza in St. Augustine functioned as a central business district. Modern buildings and storefronts occupy sites of former colonial buildings. A modest skyscraper is home to a bank and in spite of some attempt at appropriate decoration is totally out of scale with the rest of the scene (Graham, 221).

The center of the Plaza has been made into a landscaped park, not a standard feature of colonial plazas. An open air market, dating from the nineteenth century, is located in the middle, with a Confederate memorial nearby. A restored government building at the west end of the Plaza is modeled on structures of the British period, but the traffic that pours through the Plaza deals a devastating blow to this focal point of the townscape.

My sense-of-place profile analysis resulted in a composite score of −11.6 for the Plaza. This negative score, the worst for any of the three St. Augustine scenes chosen for analysis, was due to the presence there of structures and activities that are incompatible with a historic Spanish plaza. With the exception of open space that is suitable for some types of recreation, the Plaza is not suited for traditional historic landscape activity. The Plaza is a potentially grand feature of the townscape of St. Augustine, and it is the one most thoroughly desecrated. An obvious conclusion is that the symbolic message of the old Spanish Plaza is virtually inaudible. While the area is pleasantly landscaped and serves as a nice central city park, there is no special historic symbolism in the contemporary scene to suggest the past importance of the place.

St. George Street

St. George Street was the main thoroughfare into the heart of colonial St. Augustine. It extended from the city gate at the north protective wall directly to the Plaza. Such streets, in spite of their prominence, were not wide avenues in colonial times. Early Spanish residents built structures at the edges of streets with private space toward the rear of lots. The visual effect during Colonial times would have been of low buildings sitting directly on street edges and creating walled avenues.

Since colonial times St. George Street has been subjected to a number of changes. Drawings and photographs from the late nineteenth and early twentieth centuries show the same narrow street with second stories added during British occupation and later. A few commercial establishments occupied northern sections of the street, but southern blocks near the Plaza (central business district of the early twentieth century) experienced major changes. Old structures were torn down and replaced or modified to look modern.

A portion of St. George Street toward the City Gate has been designated "San Agustin Antiguo" (Fig. 4). Very few structures remain in St. Augustine from any of the colonial periods. Thus, what one sees are houses and shops reconstructed, and in some cases newly constructed, to give the appearance of a historic Hispanic façade. Overhanging balconies on second floors, iron grillwork, white walls, and tile roofs greet visitors along a narrow old street. The State of Florida program has developed a new name for identification of their exhibition area: the "Spanish Quarter." This is in imitation of the popular French Quarter of New Orleans and is an attempt to attract more visitors. However, the state intrepretive program is advertised and presented in a low-key way. Florida doesn't want to compete with private enterprise along St. George Street. Even here in

Fig. 4   St. George Street, St. Augustine. Renovation of existing
structures, and new construction, are designed to create a Spanish
Colonial façade. Entrance to the "San Agustin Antiguo" interpretive
program is on the left. During peak tourist season the street is
crowded, with commercial enterprises dominating the scene. (Photo
by author)

the historic district core the number of state-owned buildings
is fairly modest. Commercial establishments dispense an-
tiques, crafts, food, and information. Some of these establishments are better than others, and several of the restaurants
have good reputations.

On the spectrum of St. Augustine historic landscapes, northern St. George Street must be rated above the Plaza. My sense-
of-place rating for it was +7.0, the best of the three sites in St.
Augustine. This is, nevertheless, a relatively weak positive
rating. My compatibility matrix revealed that St. George Street
is primarily a recreational rather than educational environment. An observant visitor comes away with mixed feelings.
These might include an appreciation for some Hispanic architectural detail, a better understanding of Spanish Colonial life
through some exhibits, and negative feelings about the crasser
commercial establishments. Interpretive efforts on St. George
Street are lost in a kaleidoscope of sights and sounds. This is
not to say that a Williamsburg approach, with a walled-off unified presentation is any more authentic. However, one could
probably wish for a little more authenticity in a few blocks of
the city.

The Waterfront and Castillo

Most colonial administrative cities like St. Augustine are at
least partially oriented toward the sea. Harbors were the beginnings of routes back to the homeland ties that still bound the
hearts of colonial settlers. However, St. Augustine's was never
a great harbor. The shallow and narrow inlet through the beach
bar limited the kinds of ships that could pull up to the piers.
Historic drawings show small piers extending from an area
south of the fort to and beyond the Plaza. The main dock
during the nineteenth century was in the Plaza area. These
piers continued to be used by coastal shipping into the early
years of this century. The street along the waterfront, Avenida
Menendez, was a popular promenade. Elimination of important shipping to St. Augustine and routing of Florida route A1A

across the bridge from Anastasia Island and then north along the waterfront changed appearances along the harbor edge. To allow for vehicular traffic and pedestrians, the waterfront was extended into the river. On the other side of the street are a series of commercial establishments (Fig. 5).

The waterfront's principal historic feature is Castillo de San Marcos. Under control of the National Park Service, the massive Castillo performs a critical role in St. Augustine's interpretive program. Initial impressions of the Castillo as an early Spanish fortification can be somewhat misleading. When one remembers that the Castillo was finished just in time for British occupation and was then under Spanish control for the relatively short second colonial period, Castillo de San Marcos is actually better viewed as representative of more recent times. The Park Service makes this clear by explaining the fort's role in the Second Seminole War and later.

Visually, St. Augustine's waterfront is a mixture of old and new. The Castillo is a reminder of historic times, while traffic, noise, and shops prevent visitors from gaining much sense of history. I scored the waterfront as −5.6. Its greatest compatibility is for marine recreation. Pleasure craft of all sizes dock south of the Plaza, and it is fun to watch shrimp boats as they return to port in the evening.

Conclusion

St. Augustine possesses a historic townscape, but the symbolic message is unclear to most visitors. This messsage is, in fact, a reflection of the failure of leadership. One can find only minimal evidence of foresight and planning in the historic townscape. As a result St. Augustine impresses visitors as an interesting mixture of historical, commercial, and urban elements. Casual visitors are unlikely to gain much understanding of Spanish colonial life. Put another way, St. Augustine today is not a first-rate tourist or cultural environment. Perhaps an oft-

Fig. 5   Avenida Menendez, St. Augustine. Route A1A runs along a modern waterfront toward the Castillo in the background. The river walkway to the right is built on fill dredged from the river. Businesses line the other side of the street, which narrows between the Castillo and the historic district. The dominant image is that of a busy, nicely landscaped transportation route. (Photo by author)

quoted truism about people, "there is no heavier burden than a great potential," is applicable to historic sites as well. Because St. Augustine has such superior historic credentials, we expect more than we find.

Why has St. Augustine failed to develop appropriately as a historic site? Leaders from all interested constituencies—government at different levels, preservation experts, plus local citizens and business people—were unable to agree on a workable historic landscape compromise. Immediate return on commercial investment seemed more attractive than projected return on more consistent historic landscape interpretation.

Admittedly there is not likely to be an easy solution to this historic landscape management problem today. Rural, undeveloped, or tightly controlled sites can have preservation plans applied with relative ease because there are fewer challenges to vital interests. There is a sizeable existing real estate investment in St. Augustine's historic district as well as a state transportation investment (Dunkle, 1955). A spirited defense of property rights in such places would challenge preservation action.

There is some reason to hope for improvement. Some have claimed that St. Augustine failed to develop a better interpretive program in the past because this was not an Anglo-American historic townscape. Today a sizeable and growing Hispanic population in the United States, and particularly in South Florida, may rightly demand that this place, with its important vestiges of Spanish colonial heritage, be something more than just an above-average tourist trap. There are, after all, rights for all Americans to experience authentic historic landscapes associated with their heritage. Political pressure in the future should promote the continued improvement in St. Augustine's landscape.

State of Florida programs will no doubt assist in St. Augustine's preservation. The "San Agustin Antiguo" program is movement in the right direction. A first-class archeological project utilizing the professional expertise of the University of

Florida is producing results that will be useful for future interpretive efforts. One day a visitor to St. Augustine should be able to experience a pleasant urban setting preserved through interpretive programs and historic landscapes. Authentic historic townscapes will be conducive to acquiring an appreciation of Spanish and British colonial life in Florida. Legitimate commercial activities within the historic district will be conducted so as not to detract from primary messages. In short, it will be a first-class historic townscape.

5. Colonial National Historical Park, Virginia

Writing to an influential member of Congress, Kenneth Chorley, the president of Colonial Williamsburg, said of Jamestown, Williamsburg, and Yorktown, "It seems to me it can be little short of Divine Providence that these three places are within approximately fifteen miles of each other. Taken together they tell one of the world's most fascinating stories" (1948). It matters little that Chorley had goals in mind that were more human than divine. His amazement that three sites of such historic importance were to be found in this relatively restricted area on a peninsula between the James and York rivers in Virginia points to strengths and weaknesses of that region as a historic landscape (Fig. 6).

It can justly be claimed that no other area in the United States has as much right to be called the "Colonial National Historical Park." Jamestown is the site of the first efforts at permanent settlement of colonists hailing from the country that would become the predominant cultural hearth for North America. And though America's Revolutionary War went on after 1781, Washington's victory over Cornwallis at Yorktown really marked the end of the Colonial Era. Thus, Jamestown and Yorktown define an era. And Williamsburg, although not an official part of the park, is a reasonable representative of the 174 years in between the first settlement and the great battle. Williamsburg's claim to fame is as principal colonial site of the House of Burgesses, the first legislative body in the new world.

Colonial National Historical Monument was established by

Congress in 1930 to provide a fitting setting for the 150th anniversary of the British surrender at Yorktown. Colonial Park was intended to present, through interpretation of colonial landscapes, an accurate and informative image of colonial life in English North America. The period around 1930 was auspicious for recognition of the historical landscape potential of this area. In the late 1920s John D. Rockefeller had begun major investment in restoration at Williamsburg. The federal government, through the National Park Service, was taking on

Fig. 6   Colonial National Historical Park. Jamestown, Williamsburg, and Yorktown are connected by the Colonial Parkway. The Parkway is laid out so that travelers see natural landscapes reminiscent of colonial times. (Cartography Lab., Dept. of Geography, Univ. of Florida)

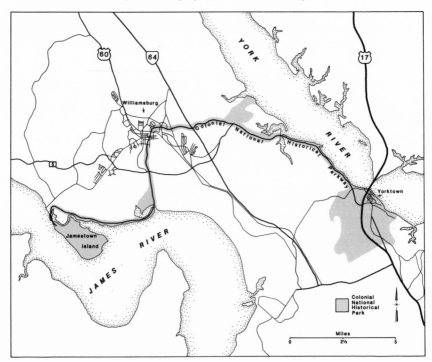

new responsibilities in the East. Formidable hurdles to be overcome included separation of sites and division of responsibility among different groups. This fragmentation has led to lack of clarity in the interpretive programs that resulted.

The Colonial National Historical Park experience is not just a story of an unusual triad of historic sites. A national commitment to major historic interpretation was developing when the park was put together. Director Horace M. Albright was leading National Park Service experts toward becoming significantly involved with eastern sites (Runte 1987). Previously their activity was almost exclusively devoted to western parks and monumental scenery. Transfer of federal property in the East to Park Service control and creation of new parks such as Colonial brought the unique professionalism of that group to the eastern seaboard.

In addition, that era witnessed the beginning of mass automobile travel. Roads were improved and large numbers of American families could afford to buy a vehicle produced on an assembly line. Places like Colonial, previously isolated and far from mass transportation facilities, were now within reach of the public. Finally, Depression-era programs, which prompted the employment of high quality workers for development of national properties, provided large numbers of professionals for interpretation and non-skilled labor for landscape and archaeological projects at Colonial. Thus, Colonial National Historical Park deserves detailed attention in an analysis of the evolution of historic landscapes in the eastern United States.

Local Historical Geography

In May of 1607 settlers arrived at Jamestown Island under a charter granted to the Virginia Company. As with other early colonists, these pioneers had a predetermined idea of the kind of site and situation they wanted for their settlement. They wanted a good harbor, a site that offered reasonable defensive characteristics, timber, water, and some open land for agriculture.

From a number of different standpoints, Jamestown Island was not an ideal settlement spot. While it offered a good anchorage and possessed natural defensive characteristics because of its separation from the mainland, it was also predominantly low-lying marsh land with little open space and would prove hard to develop. Nevertheless, "James towne" was established on the island and became the colonial capital of Virginia. The town experienced a series of disastrous fires and one rebellion during the seventeenth century. By the end of that century, as it became clear that Jamestown island was not a good place for settlement, the colonial legislature moved to nearby Williamsburg. Gradually Jamestown's population decreased until, during the eighteenth century, the island was the site of plantations and little else. Since the major significance of Jamestown is as the site of initial seventeenth-century settlement, its population decline was generally good for preservation. Rural and isolated historic landscapes are less likely to be radically altered.

Remnants of early settlement on Jamestown Island were either swept away by riverine erosion or disappeared under agricultural tillage. Of major interest at Jamestown has been the attempt to determine the exact location of 1607-era structures, which seem to have been built primarily within a wooden fort. This site of initial landings is generally agreed to be along the James River shoreline where ships could be moored in deep water. Water was deep there because the main river current ran along that shore. Presumably the fort was near this landing site. The current which produced the anchorage proceeded during the following three hundred years to wash away the old fort and its remnants. Most archaeologists have concluded that the fort was located beyond the present shoreline (Cotter 1958).

Yorktown had a somewhat different experience. Originally it was the York River termination for a log barricade erected as protection against Indians. However, as tobacco plantations began producing surpluses during the seventeenth century, requirements for a good port focused attention on maritime facilities at Yorktown. Not only did this town have a superior harbor it also was close to Gloucester Point on the opposite shore, which provided a relatively easy crossing for ferries.

The characteristics that made Yorktown initially attractive as a port were equally inviting to British General Lord Cornwallis in 1781 (Davis 1982). Having completed a long and trying southern campaign, Cornwallis needed a spot to garrison and be resupplied. Yorktown would provide protection while he waited for arrival of a British fleet. In consultation with his French allies, George Washington decided to make an all-out effort to defeat the British at Yorktown. He knew that a French fleet would attempt to blockade Chesapeake Bay and prevent British ships from reaching Cornwallis. A successful siege would force Cornwallis to surrender his command.

With the French fleet offshore, Continental forces launched a classic siege directed at the earthen fortifications surrounding Yorktown (Fig. 7). Siege tactics called for the progressive advance of offensive trenches toward parallel defensive trenches, while the attackers concentrated increasing firepower on the defenders. Eventually a series of successful attacks were launched against several British strong points called "redoubts." Failing in an attempt to evacuate to Gloucester Point because of bad weather, Cornwallis was compelled to surrender his depleted command.

In 1930 little remained of colonial Yorktown. Bypassed as a shipping point, and suffering some destruction during the Civil War, Yorktown had fewer than ten colonial structures left at the arrival of the National Park Service.

Williamsburg had a historic connection to both Jamestown and Yorktown. The site was settled in 1632 as limitations of settlement along the James became more apparent and as plantation agriculture needed more interior land. By 1698 Williamsburg had become the colonial capital. This did not mean that it was a large city. The prevalence of dispersed plantation agriculture in the tidewater region meant that most people were living in the countryside on these farms. Most commerce occurred at docks along rivers rather than in central-place locations. Administrative towns like Williamsburg remained relatively small. During legislative sessions Williamsburg was a busy place, but it was quiet the rest of the year. Increasingly volatile political times before the American Revolution found Williamsburg, as site of the House of Burgesses, a location of important thinking and decision-making by the Virginia aristocracy, who would assume leading political roles in the coming years.

Following the colonial period, Virginia's capital was moved to Richmond, and Williamsburg slipped back to being a quiet rural town of the tidewater. Larger than Yorktown, and the site of William and Mary College, Williamsburg had more colonial remnant structures than Yorktown. Some eighty-eight buildings remained from colonial times and were found in all sections of town at the start of Rockefeller restoration.

The idea of a Colonial National Historical Park would not have been complete without inclusion of land outside the three nodes of interest. Rural landscapes of the colonial tidewater were dominated by plantations, but possessed other important elements. Land was generally low lying, marshy, and heavily vegetated. Contrary to popular opinion, most structures in town and the countryside were not those of the gentry (Glassie 1975, 177). Cottages and two-story "I" frame houses were found along overland routes.

One scheme proposed during the 1930s was to use plantations as foci for a colonial park. Historian Charles W. Porter presented arguments for this idea to Park Service Director Newton B. Drury.

> In selecting Virginia as the locale for Colonial National Historical Park, Congress also obviously had in mind the commemoration of the colonial plantation culture and economy that produced

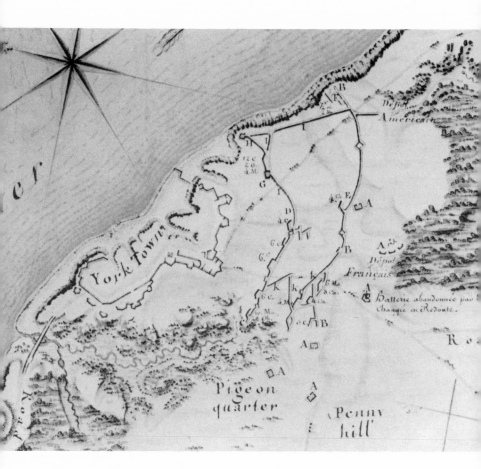

Fig. 7   Yorktown, 1781. This French map shows Yorktown and the
Battlefield. Trenches and artillery batteries surround the town on
cleared fields. (Courtesy of the Department of Rare Books, Cornell
University Library.)

the great founding fathers of this Republic—Henry, Washington, Jefferson, Madison, Mason, and Monroe, all of whom were planters. . . . If we carry out the program for Colonial National Historical Park envisioned by Congress, which included acquisition of the three outstanding plantations of the Yorktown vicinity, we can have a Colonial National Historical Park which will be superlative in quality and worthy of National Park Service standards in striving for the *superlative and best*—an exhibit able to stand on its own feet even in the presence of the work of Rockefeller at Williamsburg. (1945)

Eventually lack of funding and more than sufficient challenges at Jamestown and Yorktown would limit federal rural land ownership. The Park Service acquired acreage in the Yorktown battlefield area, and for a road to connect the three main sites. Signs along this road, Colonial Parkway, tell of important countryside activities in colonial times. However, in spite of rational arguments supporting inclusion of agrarian colonial landscapes, the park has generally treated the rural tidewater as a route between the three town sites. Plantation agriculture is not a focus of interpretation, and this is one of the key weaknesses of the park.

Plantations are a controversial theme for the Park Service. Because of the association of plantation life with slavery, questions of how to interpret this phase of our nation's history for the public is a hotly debated topic. One roadblock to accurate interpretation is that historians don't agree in their accounts of slavery. Further, how should blacks become involved in any program for interpreting plantation life? For example, Williamsburg, just down the road, has been accused of not presenting an accurate picture of conditions for black people during colonial times. Could a plantation landscape prove less controversial than these sociological or historical based programs? However it is done, there is a need for interpretation of colonial plantation life. Resolution of this general issue might clear the way for further development of historic plantation landscapes at Colonial.

Factors Affecting Landscapes
of Colonial National Historical Park

Theories of community power suggest that fundamental decisions are made through interaction among leaders. I believe that leaders share an adherence to principles guaranteed by the Constitution and that these principles provide the basis for a "landscape belief system." Acting from this basis of agreement, leaders are often able to reach compromise solutions to common historic landscape problems. This is a useful model with which to approach an analysis of the decision-making at Colonial. The disparate parts of the park were and are under different authorities. In the beginning all these people and institutions shared a limited local goal—a commitment to the preservation and effective utilization of these historic landscapes. The commitment to preserve did not include specific plans for action. Exactly how were Yorktown, Jamestown, and the area in between to be presented to the public? What sort of a relationship would the federal effort establish with existing programs at Williamsburg? Questions of this sort would occupy succeeding generations of those interested in Colonial National Historical Park.

The Williamsburg Model

In 1926 John D. Rockefeller was persuaded to underwrite restoration at Williamsburg, and the world of American historic preservation has not been the same since. Rockefeller funds contributed to Williamsburg total over 90 million dollars. Today, Williamsburg is run by the Colonial Williamsburg Foundation, a private non-profit organization with no official connection to Rockefeller philanthropy.

While the Colonial Williamsburg Foundation is engaged in various efforts involving historic research and publication, its most visible program is the 173-acre restored area in the heart of old Williamsburg. Approximately a hundred restored or replicated colonial buildings are found, along with a staff dressed in colonial garb performing various tasks designed to entertain, enlighten, and serve visitors. Vehicular traffic is severely restricted in the restored area and entirely prohibited during daylight hours.

Although Williamsburg has faced the financial challenges associated with energy crises and recession, it remains the best-known preservation of an entire historic district in the United States. The Williamsburg model, involving vast infusions of private development dollars followed by hoards of tourists, is enough to palpitate the heart of any enterpreneur/politician. Yet, among preservation professionals and scholars in the related fields of history and architecture, Williamsburg has been controversial from the beginning. For every local booster group with a historic site on its hands that dreams of producing a miniature Williamsburg, there have been individuals questioning the wisdom of aspects of that approach. It is not that Williamsburg is found totally lacking in merit; rather it is felt other approaches should be considered as well.

A fundamental criticism of Williamsburg centers on questions of realism. First, there is the issue of physical realism. That is, when 173 acres are walled off from the rest of the world, can what one experiences in such a place reflect either a past or present reality? Another issue is historical realism. Can contemporary scholars ever know enough to realistically restore a colonial town? A final issue has to do with value realism. Does a restoration like Williamsburg accurately represent the fundamental values of colonial America?

This last issue is probably the hardest to come to grips with. Value realism was discussed at Williamsburg about ten years after the beginning of restoration. In late October 1938 the renowned American architect Frank Lloyd Wright spoke about Williamsburg's restoration at William and Mary College. His unrecorded speech caused such a negative reaction among proponents of the Williamsburg effort that Wright sought to clarify his remarks through a statement released to a Richmond newspaper.

Wright began this clarification with the remark, "Were I allowed but a single criticism of Williamsburg, I should say the attempt to create an 'illusion' by way of the restoration is where the matter goes wrong and is likely to do harm . . ." (1938). That Williamsburg represented an illusion or separation from reality was, for Wright, based on a number of considerations. First, his architectural sense was offended by the fact that Williamsburg was primarily imitative construction. In his words, "We have the English version of French culture brought over to an Indian infested region—there to be named Williamsburg and be as true to back home as the English would make it." Wright saw the Williamsburg restoration as revival of a structural form that was unworthy as a symbol of the art and particularly the ideals of the new nation. His ringing criticism ends with the following: "And I repeat that were Thomas Jefferson alive today in the spirit he would stand and say more bitter and caustic things to his worshipers (I called them pall-bearers at Williamsburg) than I have the heart or the capacity to say." Criticism of Williamsburg's lack of realism has continued to the present (Leone 1981).

Williamsburg and other similar places meet a genuine nostalgic need for a sanitized view of the past. Lack of satisfaction with the present always turns people toward imagined golden ages. There is nothing wrong with meeting this need, but its lack of correspondence to reality causes worry about the quality of the messages we are receiving from our historic landscapes. City, town, and countryside were and are parts of an integrated whole. The relationship between central place and hinterland, with towns supplying needed services while rural areas yield their agricultural surpluses, prohibited their being widely separated. Furthermore, people frequently moved from farm to town and back again, establishing a strong spatial relationship that came to define the character of a place. The

Williamsburg model of preservation need not be abandoned, but its limitations should be recognized. In any case, whether praised or criticized, the prominent place that Williamsburg occupies in American preservation testifies to its importance. In comparison, one thinks of Savannah, Georgia. In a downtown built over a period of 150 years, James Oglethorpe's plan of 1733 stimulated development of grid-patterned streets and interspersed squares. While attention is given to the contemporary visitor seeking historic insight, the area remains a functioning downtown. Savannah squares and old houses have been maintained and restored, and shops have found their way into carefully preserved buildings along the waterfront. At the same time the presence of poorer housing and ordinary people lends a realistic atmosphere to the scene. The occasional art deco buildings or other incompatible structural forms are limited in size, and therefore, do not substantially affect the dominant milieu. The superficial sheen of an illusion like Williamsburg is replaced with a deeper reality in Savannah.

It can be rightly charged that this evaluation can be made today after sixty years of experience with the Williamsburg model, a period that is likely to turn up problems with any preservation approach. At the time the planners of Colonial began to think about what should be done with Jamestown and Yorktown, the Williamsburg work had only been underway for about five years, and it is therefore not surprising that one conceivable preservation model for those nearby towns was a restoration in the Williamsburg mold.

The first plans for Jamestown Island called for rebuilding some early structures. In the early 1930s the only historic structures were ruins of an eighteenth-century plantation house and remnants of a church tower. Jamestown Island was held by several owners and used mostly for agriculture. An aerial photograph from that era shows extensive agricultural fields beyond a small historic area on the riverfront (Fig. 8). That area is owned by the Association for the Preservation of Virginia Antiquities (APVA). The Park Service, after failing to negotiate a sale for the rest of the island, gained title for $165,000 through condemnation proceedings. An aerial photo from approximately twenty-five years later illustrates an intermediate stage of park development at Jamestown (Fig. 9). A frequent problem for preserved areas is the encroachment of vegetative growth. Although the later photograph is from a different angle, and from a different season of the year, the proliferation of vegetation is clearly evident. In the case of Jamestown Island, however, resurgence of vegetative cover would prove to be helpful for the interpretive program.

In the 1930s Park Service personnel felt that Jamestown Island interpretation should focus on the initial site of English settlement. There was general agreement that the site of the 1607 settlement had been eroded by the James River. A memorandum to the director of the National Park Service suggested restoring the original shoreline by dredging the river, and constructing a stockade to represent the original structure (Peterson 1931). It was also clear that any interpretive program at Jamestown would require extensive historical and archeological investigation. Research soon revealed the primitive state of knowledge concerning Jamestown. The nature of early colonial structures was unknown, and exact locations were proving hard to pinpoint. Jamestown had suffered a series of natural and human disasters which resulted in the destruction of early settlements. These were replaced by successive towns until the virtual abandonment at the end of the seventeenth century. Identification of specific settlement sites required searching through a maze of archeological evidence.

By 1940 Park Service opinion had shifted to the view that the emphasis at Jamestown should be on making the natural landscapes of the island as reminiscent as possible of those that challenged original settlers. Roads, paths, museums, archeological exhibits, and signs would be oriented toward an evocative recreation of the physical environment in 1607. J. C. Harrington, who was in charge of the archeological work at Jamestown, pointed out that any structural restoration could

Fig. 8   Jamestown Island, c 1930s. On the closest shoreline are twenty-two acres of land belonging to the Association for the Preservation of Virginia Antiquities. A rectangular enclosure includes rebuilt outlines of several early state houses, with a modern caretaker's house behind. The tall memorial to the right center is a 300th anniversary monument erected outside APVA land in 1907. The most likely location for the first settlement was near the river end of the third breakwater from the ferry pier in the background. Extensive cleared fields testify to agricultural activity on Jamestown Island at this time. (Archives, Colonial National Historical Park)

Fig. 9   Jamestown Island, c 1950s. Only one breakwater remains from the
1930s. Extensive growth of vegetation is particularly noticeable around the
old state house area and in the background along shoreline. A James River
ferry is about to land at the pier. Ferry Parking is next to the 300th
anniversary monument. The main area of archeological investigation can
be seen beyond the monument. Park development of the island is far from
complete at this point. (Archives, Colonial National Historical Park)

only be conjectural, that it would be unwise to compete with Williamsburg through a similar type of restoration program, and that there was great potential for having an interpretive program based on various archeological activities (1939a). Thus, Jamestown Island was not to go the Williamsburg route.

The decision to emphasize Jamestown's natural environment has been important to the preservation movement. Chief Park Service Historian Ronald F. Lee, in a memorandum for the director, commented on growing interest in the natural environments of historic sites (1946). A conference at Jamestown had impressed those present with the evocative nature of the physical setting. Under a section titled "Aspects of the American Scene," Lee suggested further Park Service investigation of "The elements of sound, sight, taste, smell, and feeling as factors in the total impression evoked by an historic site." Other suggested topics included: "The links between architecture and setting," "The Links between ruins and setting," "Monumentation and landscape," and "Some stable landscape elements in the American cultural scene." After only fifteen years in the East, the Park Service was moving into areas of lasting importance to the preservation of historic landscapes.

Yorktown possessed a different setting for historic development from Jamestown's, and potential for a Williamsburg-like restoration seemed greater there. A memorandum from historical assistants to the superintendent of Colonial stated: "It is still an open question whether the Park Service should attempt a development along the lines of Williamsburg restoration or merely preserve what is here and restore those few buildings needed for administrative purposes" (Gardner 1934).

The case of Yorktown was different from that of Williamsburg. The town was of later origin, and was a port rather than an administrative center. Yorktown had changed in the intervening years, particularly as a result of Civil War action, and retained few authentic colonial structures. In addition, attention at Yorktown was focused on the events of 1781, and these had been centered on the battlefield surrounding the town. For these reasons, and because the Park Service had resolved not to compete directly with the Rockefeller operation nearby, the following recommendation came forward by 1940:

> Formulation of a historical-architectural program for the old Town of Yorktown naturally leads to a consideration of the theories which apparently governed and the results which obtain in the restoration of Colonial Williamsburg, only thirteen miles distant. Regardless of the views of any single individual in respect to the soundness of the premises adopted at Williamsburg, two facts are clear. There is not unity of thought on the matter. Equally intelligent analyses reach conflicting conclusions.
>
> The very conflict of opinion invoked by the Williamsburg project is sufficient reason to avoid another development based on like theories, particularly in such close proximity to Williamsburg. Surely, another restoration-reconstruction program in the Williamsburg manner would attract far greater interest in a location distant enough from Williamsburg to give geographical breadth to the compelling influence of interpretation of this sort. (Good 1940)

Yorktown would not attempt to follow the Williamsburg model. Attention was focused on the Siege of 1781 and on the battlefield, and the Park Service was not taking the easy way out. To undertake effective development and interpretation of a historic military landscape was an innovative step.

Uniting Places and People
There were obvious differences between Colonial National Monument in the early 1930s and the typical western park of the National Park Service. In the West the Park Service controlled larger areas of land, but these larger areas of operation were normally under one organization. In addition, population densities tended to be lower, and naturalist themes associated with those places were generally supported by the public. At Colonial the total area was not all that great, but organizational jurisdictions overlapped. The countryside in tidewater Virginia was populated, albeit in an uneven fashion, and the unifying theme of the park was based on cultural and human-

istic values. Drawing historic sites and people together would prove to be a major challenge in Virginia.

At Colonial in 1930 there was plenty of motivation to get the job done. The 150th anniversary of the Battle at Yorktown was to be celebrated in 1931. Legislation was pushed through Congress in order to provide funds for the celebration and to associate the Colonial idea with that important event. Local and national elites got involved. The initial cast of leaders behind the Colonial idea included representatives from the highest levels of preservation and politics. Williamsburg interest was represented by the support of Reverend W. A. R. Goodwin, the man who has been credited with stimulating John Rockefeller to start restoration at Williamsburg, and by Kenneth Chorley, head of the Wiliamsburg restoration organization. The National Park Service interest was represented by Horace M. Albright, director of that agency. Albright and an expanded eastern parks program could soon count on support from Interior Secretary Harold Ickes and President Franklin D. Roosevelt. William E. Carson, chairman of the Virginia State Commission on Preservation and Development assumed an active role in promoting the Colonial idea. Congressman Louis Cramton from Michigan was instrumental in writing legislation authorizing the park and has been credited by some with originating the Colonial concept.

The basic idea of Colonial was that the three historic sites— Jamestown, Williamsburg, and Yorktown—would be conceptually linked through a connecting Parkway. While there was general agreement that establishment of a Colonial National Monument was a good idea, a tremendous effort was required to coordinate among the various groups and individuals representing specific interests.

An initial problem was establishment of landscape control and boundaries for the monument. The Association for the Preservation of Virginia Antiquities owned twenty-two acres of Jamestown Island that included important portions of the oldest non-eroded settlement sections on the island. Rockefeller interests owned over 90 percent of the colonial town of Williamsburg. Yorktown and the surrounding battlefield were held by an array of individual property owners. All of these groups and other citizens were interested in questions of property value and control. What were to be the implications of inclusion of a particular piece of property in the national monument to the individual or group property owner? Would freedom of choice in regard to their properties be limited by this action? These concerns touch on basic Constitutional issues.

An example of a problem that arose out of such concerns involved the issuing of a proclamation establishing Colonial National Monument in early 1931. This document included Williamsburg as part of the area involved, and it drew an immediate protest from Kenneth Chorley to the director of the National Park Service. Albright indicated in response that a proclamation was necessary to achieve funding for the sesquicentennial celebration. Further, "It was clearly understood of course that neither Mr. Rockefeller nor any of the Officers of the Williamsburg Holding Corporation had agreed to the inclusion of Williamsburg in the Monument and that no commitment whatever had been made in reference to Williamsburg becoming a part of the Monument either now or hereafter" (1931). This touchy issue has surfaced repeatedly during the intervening years. Williamsburg likes to have a federal presence on the peninsula allocating funds to enhance historic landscapes, which in turn helps Williamsburg attract more visitors. At the same time, Colonial Williamsburg jealously guards its own prerogatives. This is the equivalent in historic preservation terms of having your cake and eating it too.

Beyond divergent institutional interests there was the question of getting different people to work together. The National Park Service experienced problems when trying to obtain cooperation from professionals representing different organizations. Williamsburg was an established operation. In spite of all the Rockefeller money it was somewhat limited in scope. Architects, both structural and landscape, as well as interior decoration experts were really in charge of the Williamsburg restoration. From the National Park Service viewpoint, background research needed for thoroughly accurate restoration was not being conducted at Williamsburg. Of course, the Park Service was careful not to suggest that they would infringe on the Williamsburg work. Yet, Chorley was anxious for the Williamsburg operation to establish an advisory relationship with the Park Service. In the long run the federal government had deeper pockets than even a Rockefeller.

At the policy-making level, Chorley and Albright often expressed a desire for cooperation, but getting cooperative effort at the scene was a different matter. One obvious problem was that cooperation at Colonial was perceived by Park Service personnel to be a one-way street. That is, Williamsburg wanted to advise the Park Service but accepted little advice in return. A one-sided relationship is generally not a healthy one. For instance, there was a cooperative effort to furnish the restored Moore house at Yorktown. The Moore house was where the surrender agreement was signed, and it had been purchased by John Rockefeller before the establishment of Colonial. Subsequently the National Park Service took over, supervised its restoration, and sought to furnish it. The superintendent at Colonial requested Williamsburg advice in furnishing and decorating. This was an area in which Williamsburg had considerable expertise, and they sent several people to assist in the effort. Eventually the superintendent decided not to follow the Williamsburg advice, citing budgetary restraints. As a result a letter from Chorley to Albright stated: "I have a very distinct feeling that your people at Yorktown would rather go ahead with their own plans in accordance with what they have and the money they have to spend rather than be accurate" (1932). This perception of the state of affairs was, as could have been expected, somewhat different from that held by the National Park Service. In the Charles Hosmer interviews, Colonial Park Service employees talked about their frustration when working with Williamsburg people. Park Service workers felt that

Williamsburg personnel were snobbish, self-interested, and just wanted to restore buildings at the expense of other historical research.

Of course, as with any human organization, all was not harmonious within the Park Service. Different phases of work at Colonial were spread out at a number of sites, with archeology and archival research at Jamestown; archeology, architecture, historical research, interpretive programming, and administration at Yorktown. These various projects had been set up piecemeal by the Park Service, and lack of a clear organizational chart was to play havoc with operations. The Park Service went through two different superintendents at Colonial before finding a person who could bring some harmony to their diverse operations. It was not until the mid-1930s that an initial master plan for the entire park was adopted with clear-cut lines of authority.

Spatial separation of sites and organizational separation of authority continued to be a challenge for years at Colonial National Historical Park. In 1948, eighteen years after the founding of the park, Kenneth Chorley, who was still running Colonial Williamsburg, wrote to Congressman Bland of Virginia concerning the need for coordinating efforts. In a letter that addressed a number of issues, including a call for more federal money, Chorley suggested "that an official coordinating committee be established consisting of representatives of the National Park Service and Colonial Williamsburg to develop a well thought out, coordinated educational program for Jamestown, Williamsburg and Yorktown" (1948). Chorley's letter was forwarded by Congressman Bland to Newton B. Drury, the director of the National Park Service. His response indicated that the Park Service had always favored close coordination of efforts. Further, "This service will be glad to enter into such cooperative efforts which could be provided for either by a written understanding in an exchange of letters or by a cooperative agreement entered into under the authority of the Historic Sites Act of August 21, 1938" (1948). In the view of some professionals long associated with Colonial, there never was a unified effort between Williamsburg and Colonial for development or interpretation (Hosmer interview, Roy Appleman). Although contacts between Colonial Williamsburg and Colonial National Historical Park are friendly, there is still no official relationship.

Other relationships have proved challenging as well. The case of the Association for the Preservation of Virginia Antiquities on Jamestown Island is a good example. Twenty-two acres along the historic shoreline were owned by the APVA before creation of the park. Questions concerning the relationship of this property to the park involved delicate negotiations over a period of time. The APVA is an important organization in the state of Virginia, run by women from a number of patrician families. While it might have been logical for the Park Service to buy APVA property on Jamestown Island, there was no thought of forcing such an issue. For the first decade of Colonial's existence the Park Service explored ways to integrate the twenty-two acres into the interpretive program. This was a particularly delicate question since archeology would be a primary focus at Jamestown. The exact location of the first settlement on the island was unknown and of great interest to scientists. However, to dig in the most likely spot would involve disturbing some Confederate earthworks from the Civil War. Hence some individuals in the APVA were unwilling to permit any archeological investigation on their property (Smith 1939). J. C. Harrington, Archeologist in Charge at Jamestown, presented a plan to undertake limited investigations on APVA land (1939b). Thus, thorough archeological investigation has centered in areas further to the east. Today the APVA retains title to its twenty-two acres, an area that is partially interpreted for the public by the Park Service. The APVA receives a sizable proportion of all entrance fees collected by the Park Service on Jamestown Island, and this is said to be a major source of their annual budget.

In the 1980s, problems of overlapping jurisdictions and divided authority are more prevalent than ever. In relations with other governmental agencies, the park has to consider the needs of three counties, two municipalities, a large Naval Weapons Depot on the York River, a nearby Central Intelligence Agency training facility, and two state of Virginia tourist centers. Additionally, private capital has constructed numerous attractions nearby to draw on the tourist market. There is an obvious need for professional planners in the Park Service.

Historic Landscapes of Colonial National Historical Park

This park, separated in space and by interpretive mode, presents a number of different historic landscapes to its visitors. A key question is how these different landscapes fit under the overarching umbrella of the Colonial Park concept.

Colonial Parkway

The need for some form of transportation between major sites in the park was foreseen during the initial founding discussions in the late 1920s. In a different era some form of mass transportation might have been considered. At Colonial the intent was to create a motor highway, an idea that has some disadvantages from the standpoint of planning a historic landscape. Since every car moves at a different pace and riders choose their own destinations, interpretive programs at sites involving automobiles have greater difficulty trying to anticipate individual choices. In addition, use of modern automobiles to negotiate colonial landscapes hardly seems fitting. In spite of these limitations, planners at Colonial laid out a remarkable roadway. This task was not simple. Land acquisition plans called for cutting a five-hundred-foot swath across the peninsula and building a tunnel under the restored colonial village at Williamsburg.

Then limited funding delayed completion of the Parkway for several decades. Perhaps the most amazing aspect of this roadway, and one that should be considered at other places, is that the route chosen was designed with views of the landscape in mind. As far as possible, travelers were to pass through undisturbed scenes, such as might have existed during colonial times. The planners laid out a route of approach to Jamestown

Fig. 10   Colonial Parkway. A pebbled concrete surface, minimal road markings, historical signs, and lush vegetation stimulates contemplation of colonial times in a natural setting. This road provides an unusual and pleasant experience for the harried automobile traveler of today. (Photo by author)

Island along a historic road with the primitive island silhouette in the distance. In consideration of the integrity of this approach, construction on the island was to be confined to inconspicuous locations.

A trip along the Colonial Parkway today is one of the most enjoyable experiences available to the motorist (Fig. 10). The surface of the road is pebbled concrete with no painted lines. Directional signs are few, and historic markers are found at conveniently located scenic turn-offs. Speed is strictly controlled at forty-five miles per hour. Thus, the traveler to Jamestown or Yorktown along the Colonial Parkway gets a fine view of tidewater historic landscapes.

However pleasant to travel, the Colonial Parkway does not provide as much of an integrating function in the Colonial landscape experience as it might. Visitors to Colonial tend to take overnight accommodations in the Williamsburg area. Thus, travelers go either to Jamestown in one direction or Yorktown in the other. In addition, numerous tourist attractions have developed in the area on a series of modern roads and highways. With approximately 2 million visitors to the area each year, perhaps it is just as well that the Parkway is not used by all.

Jamestown

A decision was made at Jamestown in the early 1930s to emphasize preserving the physical landscape as it might have been found in 1607. The "new towne" area of settlement from later in the seventeenth century is mowed and contains archeological exhibits (Fig. 11). The area conveys a strong sense of the densely forested, wetland setting first utilized by English colonists (Fig. 12). A narrow automobile road passes historical markers at turn-offs. A relatively, small part of the island is devoted to a visitor's center, a glass-blowing area, and parking.

Since there are few historic structures on Jamestown Island, the landscape does not convey any sense of activity or purpose

Fig. 11 Jamestown "New Towne," 1988. Results of archeological investigations in the 1930s and 1940s are indicated by white bricks built on top of foundations of seventeenth-century structures. Paths and fences help visitors locate house lots. Signs and recordings provide information. This landscape is only suggestive of early settlement. (Photo by author)

associated with early settlement. There is little attempt at interpretation of colonial human landscapes. This aspect of the Jamestown experience has to come through exhibits and interaction with park personnel. A 1979 survey conducted by the Park Service found that almost half of the visitors had difficulty understanding the Jamestown experience in terms of commonplace seventeenth-century life. Thus, a visit to Jamestown today becomes primarily a natural landscape experience, valuable for the purpose of understanding what challenges

Fig. 12   Jamestown Island Natural Landscape, 1988. With scenes like this, the Park Service has endeavored to give visitors a sense of how the natural settings must have looked in 1607. This view from a wooden walkway to the visitors center suggests the kinds of challenges that were faced by settlers. (Photo by author)

Fig. 13   Yorktown Battlefield. Reconstructed trenches, American in the foreground and British in the background, are identified by flags and a few artillery pieces. This land was cleared by the Park Service to recreate a sense of its condition in 1781. Although roads cross the battlefield, this scene is an effective interpretive tool. (Photo by author)

must have existed for initial colonial settlement. It should be noted that other nearby attractions attempt to fill this interpretive void.

Yorktown

Yorktown's mission within the interpretive program is more limited in scope than Jamestown's. Every interpretive element is supposed to revolve around the events of 1781. The other aspects of Yorktown, as colonial port city and trade center, are subordinated to the battle. In 1930 Yorktown was still a small, sleepy town on the banks of the York River that had not grown much since colonial times. The surrounding countryside, where armies had been located in 1781, was divided into a number of land holdings of different acreage and was a not particularly prosperous farming landscape in 1930. A fear of commercial development prompted Colonial planners to immediately start acquiring battlefield land.

A number of maps are available showing troop locations on the battlefield of 1781 (see Fig. 7). Since this was classic siege warfare, positions were much more static than those on a typical Civil War battlefield. The climactic action of the battle involved French and American attacks on British redoubts 9 and 10 on the night of October 14, 1781. Success with those attacks allowed the allies to complete their siege line and bombard Cornwallis into surrender.

The Park Service planned to consolidate its holdings on a major portion of the battlefield and reconstruct trenches and redoubts. Extensive clearing of vegetation was necessary. Research on trench construction and location allowed the Park Service to recreate something resembling the battlefield landscape of 150 years before (Fig. 13). Military positions are indicated by mounds of earth and a few strategically placed cannon. Signs and flags assist interpretation for visitors. A visitor to Yorktown today can stop at two exhibit centers to view displays, listen to rangers, and follow a self-guided tour of the battlefield. Because of its relative simplicity, the reality of a battle is more easily conveyed by witnessing the scene where it occurred than is the complexity of early colonial life, which is much more difficult to grasp merely by viewing the natural landscape at Jamestown.

The landscape of the battlefield at Yorktown is a human landscape modified for the purpose of siege warfare. The openness of the scene, a comparatively vast panorama, and lack of outside distraction, effectively convey a picture of the battle and its importance in the context of the American Revolution. If there is any problem with this focus on military action, it is that little attention is directed to the larger historical context. Thus, a visitor is not prompted to consider issues such as colonialism, nationalism, international relations, and the implications of all of these for the quality of life of the common citizen.

Williamsburg
Although not under the jurisdiction of Colonial National Historical Park, Williamsburg is certainly a large part of the historic landscape experience for those who visit this area. Williamsburg had an advantage over the other major sites, in that historical development at Williamsburg was independently financed and controlled by an organization that could give its full attention to that task. The national park, in comparison, was and is a creation of the federal government with all the limitations entailed in that relationship. While Williamsburg could move swiftly in any chosen direction, Colonial National Historical Park was operating within a massive system that drew its funds from Congress and had to consider actions at any single park within the context of an entire system.

The overall goal of developing historic landscapes was the same at all three sites: to aid the interpretation of colonial life and times. However, the immediate goals and methods differed significantly between Colonial and Williamsburg. As has been suggested, Williamsburg laid great stress on the reconstruction of structures, sometimes at the expense of other aspects of the landscape. Colonial was a more slow-moving operation that demanded broad background research and that chose to emphasize a natural landscape and a particular battle.

Most important in terms of differences, Williamsburg could maintain controlled admission and generate income through ticket sales to support a relatively large staff. Williamsburg advertises widely and makes a conscious effort to entertain as well as inform its visitors. A result of this distinctive effort is the unique experience historic landscape visitors have along Duke of Gloucester Street (Fig. 14). One tremendous advantage

Fig. 14   Duke of Gloucester Street, Williamsburg. Renovated and rebuilt colonial structures line a spacious street with shops, historic presentations, costumed guides, and pleasant landscaping. The atmosphere of Williamsburg stresses entertainment and action. It is the prototype of this approach to preservation. (Photo by author)

of Williamsburg is the spacious dimensions of the town plan as laid out in colonial times. The wide main street, when blocked to traffic, allows free movement and lessens a sense of contemporary human interaction, even with large crowds. Although there are congested places and times at Williamsburg, one generally has enough personal space to interact with the environment, rather than just concentrating on one's movement through a crowd. The size of the area, approximately one mile long and one-quarter mile wide, with authentic-looking structures in every direction, gives visitors a feeling of moving in a colonial environment. Craftsmen, performers, servants, and tradespeople dressed in authentic costume provide information as well as a sense of activity. On the other hand, the smell of privies, chicken coops, and pig sties does not waft through the air, and if Jefferson were set down blindfolded he would not know the place.

Williamsburg can be criticized for its spatial isolation and the lack of authenticity of certain aspects of its recreated landscape. However, this extremely active human landscape does provide a unique, entertaining, and potentially informative experience for visitors.

Conclusion

From a perspective of community power, the Colonial experience has illustrated how landscape preservation agreements among leaders frequently face hurdles when implemented by individuals with less authority. In founding the park, leaders of national reputation and authority supported the Colonial idea. The result was federal authorization and funding. Once the park was established, compromise deteriorated. Rockefeller and federal agency leaders were never able to formulate a unified plan that would garner overall support. The founding compromise was more successful than the operational compromise. Put another way, it is easier to achieve agreement at the top than at the bottom.

Colonial National Historical Park does not consider itself to be a primary destination of tourist travel. This suggests that the park has not been as successful as was hoped at its founding. It is certainly not as successful as a park ought to be that interprets the first 150 years of American history. The primary reason for this situation is that Williamsburg dominates the tourist market. One can argue that if Williamsburg had not developed independently, the area would not draw visitors in any significant numbers. Nevertheless, it is clear that the spatial separation of sites is paralleled by organizational separation.

Because Colonial Williamsburg is the focus of most tourist trips, relations between the park and Williamsburg are bound to be of primary concern to the intrepetive program. Kenneth Chorley indicated that at one time the Rockefeller organization had contemplated turning Williamsburg over to the Park Service. It is interesting to speculate on how such an action might have affected the Colonial situation. Perhaps two large organizations dedicated to interpreting the colonial period are too much for one small peninsula. An organizationally unified Colonial might have done a better job.

In the case of Colonial, leaders from the highest levels of government and private enterprise were faced with an extremely complex conceptual framework. Introduction of different institutional structures only increased the challenge. The superintendent of Colonial acknowledges there have been problems associated with fully realizing the unified Colonial landscape concept (Maeder 1986). Other complex historic landscapes will be developed in the future, and they should be approached with an awareness of the challenge, and with as clear-cut and undivided lines of authority as possible.

6. Sackets Harbor,
New York

St. Augustine and Colonial National Historical Park are the sites of nationally recognized historic landscapes. Places possessing less well-known historic landscapes nonetheless have to confront the same sorts of problems in dealing with landscape development and utilization. Sackets Harbor is such a place. Although it was an important port on Lake Ontario and a scene of significant military confrontation during the War of 1812, its reputation as a site of historic interest is primarily limited to New York State. In spite of this limited recognition, Sackets Harbor has a full complement of challenges to historic landscape development.

In a comparison of Sackets Harbor with the sites just analyzed, two significant differences stand out. First, as a place of more limited recognition and development potential, Sackets Harbor preservation has not attracted the attention of national leaders. In Virginia, leaders of a Rockefeller organization combined with congressmen and members of the National Park Service to provide an initial thrust for development. The concerns of both local elites and everyday citizens were somewhat submerged in the rush to start Colonial. No comparable level of leadership interest has emerged in the case of Sackets Harbor. Historical development there has had to contend with a broader range of competing local leadership and citizen interests. Second, Colonial and St. Augustine experienced initial development at a period of less restrictive governmental regulation. Red-tape challenges at Sackets Harbor in the 1970s and 1980s, when preservation efforts there were initiated, were much greater than at similar places in the 1930s. Regulatory hurdles are virtually universal for historic landscape development today.

Thus, historic landscape development at Sackets Harbor provides a contrast in terms of scope and period to the landscape evolution studies in the last two chapters. In fact, the Sackets Harbor experience is more apt to be like that confronting most locations today when they try to enhance their local historic landscape resources.

Local Historical Geography

Following the American Revolution, upstate New York became a focus of settlement interest. Unsettled land east of the Appalachian Mountains was severely limited. The Hudson River–Mohawk River–Ontario Lowland route was an easy passage to the trans-Appalachian country, and the attention of New Englanders, Revolutionary War veterans, and land speculators was drawn to the West. Some western lands were reserved for special groups, and land speculation ran rampant. Sackets Harbor is to the north of that historic east-west axis across the state, on the northeast shore of Lake Ontario. This extreme northern location may have accounted for the sparse settlement there before the beginning of the nineteenth century.

However, Sackets Harbor's value as a strategic location became obvious after the start of hostilities with England in 1812. Its importance as a military base was enhanced by an excellent anchorage at the mouth of the Black River. The British based their operations just across Lake Ontario. Since control of the Great Lakes was a strategic goal of the War of 1812, Sackets Harbor was bound to be an important port for American naval interests. It is the only harbor of any significant value on the eastern end of the lake. The port's value was somewhat offset by its isolation, for it was extremely difficult to get supplies overland. The customary route was to follow the Mohawk River to Lake Ontario at Oswego, and then ferry goods northward.

By 1812 Sackets Harbor, which had been settled for approximately ten years, included a small village centered on the port, and was home station for the only American warship on Lake Ontario. A principal port for the English was at Kingston, just thirty-five miles across the Lake. American naval power on Lake Ontario grew during the war, while the British, with extended supply lines, were trying to maintain control (Mahon 1972). In the space of a few years Sackets Harbor went from being a good but isolated port to becoming a major military installation. By the end of the war one third of all American naval forces were stationed at Sackets Harbor (Ernest 1984, 7).

The juxtaposition of Kingston and Sackets Harbor on this strategic landscape led to armed assaults on Sackets Harbor. Both military engagements at Sackets Harbor ended inconclusively. On July 19, 1812, while American power was in the initial stage of development, a British fleet from Kingston appeared offshore and bombarded the harbor and fortifications. Guns from an American brig were hauled to land and used as shore batteries. This exchange was broken off without serious consequences to either side.

By the next spring American power had grown. In addition to purchased and constructed ships, over eight thousand men were stationed at Sackets Harbor (Fig. 15). The balance of power was shifting on Lake Ontario. When American forces were dispatched for action at the western end of the Lake, the British decided to attack Sackets Harbor a second time. British ships arrived with twelve hundred men on May 28, 1813. A landing did not take place until the next day, by which time American officers had called together a force of slightly fewer than a thousand members of a citizen's militia. The action involved an initial British advance northward along the shore to the main American barracks area, followed by stiffening resistance

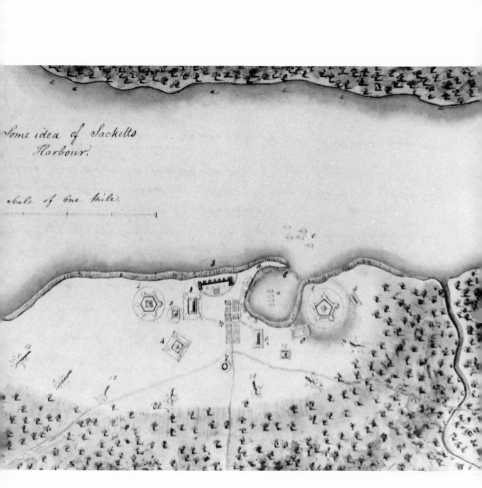

Some idea of Sacketts
Harbour.

Scale of One Mile.

Fig. 15   Sackets Harbor, 1813. This British map of Sackets Harbor
from the period of conflict is titled, "Some Idea of Sacketts
Harbour." The lack of precision in the title suggests that the map
was compiled from intelligence reports rather than observation
(Larrabee, 1968). The map gives a good idea of relative position. The
harbor, Navy Point, and the village are surrounded by fortifications.
In truth, many forts on this map were little more than earthen
trenches. (Courtesy of the Royal Ontario Museum, Toronto, Canada)

and counterattack on the British right flank. In late afternoon the British withdrew, but not before confusion among American officers had led to the self-destruction of most American supplies and several U.S. ships. It was hardly a glorious day for either side.

By the summer of 1813 American control of Lake Ontario was secure. Sackets Harbor entered a period of development as an important post on the border of an unfriendly colonial power. Both naval and land forces needed to expand their facilities to accommodate additional men and ships. Temporary quarters, then located on the battlefield, were not adequately providing for the thousands of soldiers stationed there.

Fig. 16   Sackets Harbor. In some development plans, the three segments of Sackets Harbor's historic landscape—battlefield, village and barracks—would be connected by a pathway paralleling the shore. (Cartography Lab., Dept. of Geography, Univ. of Florida)

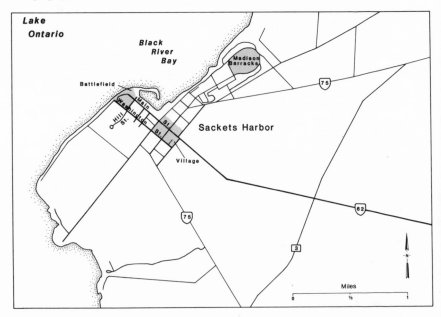

Although tension along the Canadian border was gradually reduced to an insignificant level during the nineteenth century, once a military building program got underway, it continued on its own momentum. The thrust of early nineteenth-century construction created functional zonation at Sackets Harbor. The north end of the battlefield and associated land next to the harbor became a naval base. On the other side of the village the government began construction of a major army base. Started in 1816, Madison Barracks covered over a hundred acres and grew to include many permanent structures.

The naval presence at Sackets Harbor came to an end during the 1880s. Two stone houses on the north end of the battlefield are all that remain from navy occupation. This area was deeded to the state of New York in 1933. On the other side of the village, Madison Barracks continued to serve as an Army base until the end of World War II.

A comparison of the historic resources of Sackets Harbor with lists of criteria for sites being considered as preservation projects confirms the worthiness of its landscapes. For instance, the scale of Sackets Harbor, with a historic district of about one mile by a few hundred yards, allows people to walk past one- and two-story structures ranging from old homes to museums, thereby enjoying a variety of historic landscape experiences. The village certainly has a traditional appearance and romantic associations with a heroic past. Further, its architectural elements can be blended harmoniously to create satisfying scenic views, which could be improved through appropriate modification of the landscape.

Sackets Harbor found itself at the beginning of the 1980s with three historic landscapes—battlefield, village, and barracks—that could be linked together to provide a holistic landscape experience (Fig. 16). The challenge, as at so many other places, is to develop a historic landscape that offers a unified symbolic image for visitors.

Factors Affecting Landscapes at Sackets Harbor

Economic motives are a prime stimulus for developing the historic landscapes of Sackets Harbor. The "North Country" of New York is an economically depressed region due to a decline in its agricultural economy and the failure of the St. Lawrence Seaway to bring significant economic growth to the region. Small villages like Sackets Harbor have suffered. Only as commuter communities have they managed to hold their own. Being close to Watertown, Sackets Harbor has a commuting population. However, this type of activity can do little to revitalize the economic base of a village.

A partial panacea to the town's economic decline is seen in the tourist trade. However, thus far, in spite of possessing considerable historic resources, Sackets Harbor has not become a significant tourist destination. For instance, it is estimated that 42,500 visitors came to the village during 1982. This number is thought to represent about 2.5 percent of the East Lake Ontario–Thousand Island region tourist traffic. Various recreational studies have suggested that there is a large tourist population potentially interested in Sackets Harbor. Fifty-eight million people live within three hundred miles of the village, including many Canadians. The village is readily accessible from major highways that pass nearby. Further, because the Northeast is highly urbanized, many potential visitors can be easily reached by advertising.

To tap this potential market and increase the number of visitors Sackets Harbor must become better known for the quality of its recreational experience. Many studies of the village in recent years agree that the present developmental level of historic resources will not suffice to increase the tourist trade. If Sackets Harbor can get its act together, primarily by uniting its separate historic landscapes under an exciting conceptual umbrella, its reputation could attract visitors. An obstacle to this development, however, is the seeming inability of local leaders to work together.

Establishing Preservation Priorities

A review of historic resource development at Sackets Harbor suggests that the old saying "too many cooks spoil the broth" applies to preservation as well. Many well-meaning individuals and groups have recognized preservation potential at Sackets Harbor and attempted to act, only to be bogged down in a morass of competing ideas and challenges.

The state of New York has owned most of the battlefield since 1933, but little was done to improve the site. Although the state has taken a more active interest in recent years, the battlefield remains conceptually undeveloped and a relatively poor tourist attraction. State agencies in the area have recognized a need for economic development at Sackets Harbor and responded by proposing various plans. With state stimulation the village created a historic district in 1974, encompassing almost all the built area. Creation of such a district was a prerequisite for attracting state preservation funding.

Although state efforts to develop the battlefield have been less than spectacular, that end of the village is assured continued funding and development. If Madison Barracks experiences significant revitalization, the village in the middle would certainly benefit. Since being declared surplus, Madison Barracks has been owned by different groups as an investment or for development. Use of the barracks as a housing project and then as a center for homeless families was considered, loudly opposed by the conservative local community, and rejected in the early 1970s. Village residents have shown a clear preference for private capital development of the barracks area into a commercial, residential, and recreational area. But in a period of forty years, very little has been accomplished. The future of this hundred-acre tract, with its many historic structures, is widely recognized as being closely linked to the future of the village.

An ideal solution seemed to be at hand when Frank A. Augsbury, Jr., of nearby Ogdensburg purchased the Barracks in 1978 and announced a multiphase plan for development. In his proposal, barracks housing areas would gradually be restored as apartments and condominiums, while major structures would be converted for business and civic use. One consultant for the Augsbury Corporation said that a specialized store area at the barracks could be like a small-scale Williamsburg. The Augsbury proposal was not, strictly speaking, the effort of a single man, but the design of a corporation controlled by Mr. Augsbury. His corporations were involved in a wide range of economic operations including a large oil business, shipping, real estate, and a tourist attraction known as Waterfun Village. By 1980 some restored housing was nearing completion at the barracks, but problems were on the horizon. Interest rates rose, making investment money more difficult to obtain. Oil industry organizations were starting to feel the pinch of an oil surplus, and Augsbury corporations were no exception. To make matters worse, Waterfun Village turned out to be a big money loser.

By 1982 Augsbury organizations were experiencing serious financial difficulties. They sought to save themselves through a complicated deal that would give part of the barracks to local government in exchange for tax relief on Waterfun Village. The extreme complexity of the financial arrangements of the Augsbury corporations, including their use of government-issued tax exempt bonds to support part of the renovation work, meant that most of their North Country projects were linked together. Failure of one could doom all. While Augsbury and various governmental officials looked in all directions to salvage different projects, citizens around Sackets Harbor were expressing reservations about accepting property in exchange for tax relief. These complicated maneuvers failed, the Augsbury organizations went into bankruptcy, and development stopped at Madison Barracks. A few restored apartments, several businesses along the waterfront, and grounds maintenance were the end result of Augsbury's eight-year ownership of Madison Barracks.

By the mid-1980s economic conditions in the North Country were slightly improved, due in part to a decision by the Department of Defense to permanently locate an army division at nearby Fort Drum. In September 1986 the relevant Augsbury corporation, under court bankruptcy protection, sold Madison Barracks to a group known as the Jobco Corporation. This corporation has announced plans for a 35-million-dollar barracks renovation project, at least partly funded by tax exempt bonds issued by local government. Thus, another round in the complicated attempt to redevelop Madison Barracks begins in much the same manner as the last one did.

The Sackets Harbor experience illustrates how difficult it is to select programs for the economic development of historic resources. Even in an area where one particular resource stands out as an obvious choice for development, multitudinous routes toward that goal are available. Historic resource programs have to contend with legal requirements, government agencies, private investors, and citizen's groups. Even after programs are initiated, success is anything but guaranteed. In the case of Sackets Harbor the assistance of state agencies to help plan and formulate proposals and to deal with private investors has been of critical importance. Small villages seldom have the necessary expertise or research funding to establish effective development priorities.

Governmental Initiative

In the past when the federal government or a national corporation or prominent individual were committed to a historic resource development project, the momentum created by elite stimulus was usually enough to guarantee some success. Today, however, Washington is cutting back on programs of this type, and few philanthropic organizations or corporations are willing to commit significant funding to a single site. By default, state governments have been forced to stimulate historic resource development. We have reviewed the example of St. Augustine, where, faced with entrepreneurial chaos, the state of Florida decided to participate in a minor way with the "San Agustin Antiguo" program of interpretation in the historic district. The state of Virginia has gotten involved at Colonial with their own visitor's centers.

In the case of Sackets Harbor, a need for development stimulation has been painfully obvious to state officials. The state of New York already has a vested interest through ownership of the battlefield. Further, economic welfare of such villages is of considerable concern to politicians. The key question is, in what way should state government become involved? One method is to offer inducements to local governments, and the state of New York has used such financial carrots. If local communities cooperate in specific ways they become eligible to apply for state funds to support resource development. These funding opportunities are guaranteed to get the attention of local officials. State funds create jobs.

In addition, New York has tried to encourage adoption of appropriate local ordinances to support historic programs. New York has found that there are two useful approaches to historic resource development regulations. First, under the authority of police powers, local communities are asked to pass rules governing the use of land and structures within historic districts, an area which, as in the case of Sackets Harbor, can cover an entire community. Second, the state can provide funds for professional consulting and the acquisition of property. To participate in state programs the communities must adopt approved preservation regulations and cost sharing.

A New York State effort to assist development of some specific historic landscapes, called the Urban Cultural Parks Act (New York Senate S. 776-C), was passed in 1977 and amended in 1981. This law was intended to broaden the concept of a park to include "an amalgam of historic, natural and architectural resources embracing man's total surroundings." Thirteen sites in New York were designated as possible urban cultural parks.

One was Sackets Harbor, identified in the act as "the cohesive geographical area of the village of Sackets Harbor, Jefferson County, associated with and revealing of the community's role as the headquarters for the defense of the American northern frontier."

The introduction to this legislation indicated that previous attempts to develop such places had often failed: "Despite the opportunities identified in such planning process and the commitment of local citizens and governmental bodies, significant historic settings may be jeopardized. Coordinated state and local action is needed to derive the many benefits possible for present and future generations from these historic settings." Coordinated action is the key. In other words, the legislature recognized that local efforts were floundering in the muck of conflicting goals and beliefs. Therefore, New York was saying: consolidate your goals and the state will provide guidance and some funding. In order to participate in this program, those responsible for designated urban cultural park areas were required to have completed a "management plan" within three years. This plan could be in a number of different forms, all tending toward stimulating historic revitalization efforts. If the management plans were approved by the state, the urban cultural park area would become eligible for financial assistance.

A New York State agency, the St. Lawrence–Eastern Ontario Commission, had spearheaded the effort to get Sackets Harbor into the Urban Cultural Parks Program. In response, local citizens and governmental groups began the process of establishing a management plan. Local advisory committees were formed, and feasibility studies begun. The boundaries of the urban cultural park were to include the battlefield and barracks as well as the village. These efforts resulted in a *Village of Sackets Harbor Urban Cultural Management Plan* as well as a companion Waterfront Revitalization Program (St. Lawrence–Eastern Ontario Commission 1985). The document itself is over two hundred pages and is divided into six phases. The phases cover topics such as conceptual development, planning, preservation assessment, program development, budgets, visitor projections, and environmental impact.

A number of elements of this plan deserve further scrutiny because of their potential relevance to similar efforts elsewhere. Of particulate note is that the plan recognized the need for a complete survey of the historic district as a base for further action. The survey included maps of entry points, theme areas, and scenic views. Every structure was inventoried and mapped. Buildings were classified into five categories, from "pivotal" (essential to the plan) to "incompatible." Unfortunately, a number of private residences near the battlefield park fall into this later category. Guidelines for the local planning board suggested standards for dealing with structures, including demolition of incompatible ones. A proposed park pathway, called "Harbor Walk," was shown on a map with accompanying pen-and-ink drawings of scenic views along the way. Similar drawings of street scenes showing examples of preservation improvements are extremely effective.

A crucial section—as it would be for all communities—is that dealing with budgets. This highlights a significant problem for Sackets Harbor. State and federal programs often require matching funds from local government. Yet, the village's capacity to contribute meaningfully to such development is not clear. For instance, between July 1982 and January 1984 $550,000 was put into capital improvements in the historic district. Of that amount only $18,000 came from the village budget. Projected budgets indicate that if the entire plan were to be realized over an eight-year period, local government would have to come up with approximately $3 million of a total outlay of $23 million.

It is notoriously difficult to project accurately how many visitors a historic site will draw. Weather, economic climate, highway conditions, and competing opportunities are just a few influential factors that cannot be foreseen or controlled by local communities. Nevertheless, people need to have some hope that their efforts for improvement will result in tangible economic benefits. So visitor projections are part of any plan. In the case of Sackets Harbor around fifty thousand visitors came to the battlefield in 1983 and were estimated to have spent less than three dollars each in the village. In part this lack of expenditure is due to the fact that there are not many opportunities for spending money. The plan projects there will be 250,000 visitors to Sackets Harbor by the eighth year with each spending an average of fourteen dollars.

In summary, the *Urban Cultural Management Plan* for Sackets Harbor is an impressively complete document, full of detailed agendas for improving the presentation of local historic landscapes. The unanswered question is whether or not local leaders have the capacity to implement the plan. Based on experiences to date, it is a question that should be asked.

Historic Landscapes of Sackets Harbor

Sackets Harbor's three main areas and their constituent landscapes stand separately. Many years of effort to restore and effectively utilize the battlefield, village, and barracks have borne some fruit, and improvements can be noticed in each area. However, there is still much left to be done before the historic landscapes of Sackets Harbor present an image that is in harmony with overall goals of the Urban Cultural Parks Act.

Sackets Harbor Battlefield
The battlefield portion of the cultural park has passed through many hands since the War of 1812. Parts of the area were used as agricultural land and as an informal park area for the village during the mid-nineteenth century. The navy maintained a base on the north end toward the harbor. By the end of the American Civil War, relations with Canada had eased, eliminating the need for a continued naval presence. The navy dismantled much of their base in the early 1880s. In 1886 most of the battlefield was turned over to Jefferson County. The county

deeded this land to the state of New York in 1933 to support creation of a state historic site.

A concerted effort to get the battlefield into condition for public utilization was undertaken in the 1960s. The navy turned over their remaining property to the state, which undertook a major program of archeological investigation to support interpretive programs and developed plans for additional property acquisition. In 1972 New York purchased the Union Hotel, a nineteenth-century structure near the battlefield that is used as a museum.

New York is a large and populous state with many public-owned historic sites and limited funds for their improvement. Any criticism of the slow pace at which change has come at Sackets Harbor Battlefield must be tempered by this realization. In 1984 the state produced a battlefield master plan (Ernest 1984). The plan notes difficulties at the site and a general lack of development. It contemplates no major changes, but proclaims an interest in developing four separate areas (Battlefield Farm toward the south, the central park area, Navy Point next to the harbor, and the Union Hotel along Main Street) while focusing on a theme of nineteenth-century navy life. In light of a noticeable lack of progress with the interpretation program in recent years, the master plan seems hopelessly ambitious.

The State Battlefield Historic Site includes twenty-six acres, most of which are in a narrow area parallel to the shoreline. Historic landscape interpretation is hampered by limited grounds and poor landscaping (Fig. 17). Post–World War II ranch-style houses, allowed because of a lack of appropriate zoning regulations, back up to the site and are highlighted by rows of trees. Unbelievably, this inappropriate rectangle of vegetation was reinforced during 1987 by additional plantings to replace lost trees. Signs in various locations identify points of interest, but many visitors fail to grasp details of the military action. A particular strength of the historic site is its shoreline scenery (Fig. 18). Since both battle engagements, the offshore bombardment of 1812 and the invasion of 1813, were focused on the shore zone, efforts need to be made to direct attention toward that area and away from the nonconforming structures to the rear.

A limited survey of site visitors in 1979 indicated that almost half had come specifically to see the battlefield or associated museums. As more tourists who are less knowledgeable about the site come to Sackets Harbor, the interpretive program, including battlefield landscape, will need improvement. Instead of dividing an already-fragmented interpretive program, the state should consider emphasizing the focal point of greatest public interest—the military action of 1813. By screening offensive and incompatible uses next to the park, eliminating the rectangular tree grove, doing away with a road across the battlefield, and directing public attention along the length of the historic site from Horse Island to Navy Point, the interpretive program could evolve naturally and effectively over a period of years.

The Village
Economic and demographic trends have influenced preservation action in the Village of Sackets Harbor. The 1970s were a period of recession in the North Country region. Madison Barracks was an unoccupied parcel of land on the shoreline. Village economic activity had decreased so that the only businesses were a few convenience store, restaurant, bar, and service station operations. Village population declined by 15 percent. The townscape of the mid-1980s is one of a fairly typical New York rural village (Fig. 19). Obvious signs of the lackluster economic conditions abound, and the businesses are in relatively unattractive settings along Main Street. Surrounding Main Street are some extremely attractive old homes down side streets. These create something of a New England village ambiance.

Most villagers seem to agree that the village should be more than a bedroom community for nearby Watertown. Building a business base in the village would benefit everyone, and if that

Fig. 17 Sackets Harbor Battlefield. This view is from an area near Fort Kentucky looking toward Navy Point in the direction of the British attack. A maintenance barn and tractor are in the middle of the park. Visitors are perplexed by poor interpretive design throughout the battlefield park. Improvement could be made by developing this area in the Yorktown fashion, with trenches, artillery, position markers, and vegetative control. (Photo by author)

Fig. 18 Battlefield Shoreline. Spectacular views from the edge of the battlefield park toward Black River Bay and Lake Ontario need to be highlighted in development plans. Since battle action in 1813 paralleled the shore, these two pivotal features of the park should be used to orient, educate, and please visitors. (Photo by author)

can be done through a preservation plan, which is the basis of the Urban Cultural Parks idea, then the plan would receive general support.

Many local groups have ideas about development. These include the village board, the chamber of commerce, several historical societies, review boards for development and planning, a preservation foundation, firemen's and American Legion organizations, and governmental agencies at the county and state level. One can argue that the village represents a true pluralist system.

As with most development plans, any effort at Sackets Harbor will necessarily involve placing limitations on individual freedoms in order to achieve a common goal. Such limitations are always controversial. In addition, rural villages contain strongly conservative elements that resist change of any sort. Negative reaction to "outsiders" is not uncommon, even if the intruders are trying to assist development of an economic base. When lines of communication break down, regulations are pronounced "Kremlin-like." Furthermore, years of talk with little action leave a residue of cynicism in even enthusiastic residents.

There is a great need for active articulation of landscape preservation needs in the context of Constitutional principles. The regulation of land use is more likely to be supported if it is shown to be in accord with Constitutional principles. Several public officials familiar with the village have suggested that there has been some change in local perception of historic landscape development efforts. While admitting that there is opposition, these individuals claim to detect acceptance and mild enthusiasm among most citizens.

Plans for revitalization of the village call for improvement of public areas near the waterfront. Building renovation and landscaping are proposed for Main Street. The assumption is that these developments will go hand in hand with improvement at the battlefield and Madison Barracks. Such improvements will increase tourist traffic and opportunities for local businesses.

If there is one area that has blossomed in recent years it is the harbor. There are presently six marinas, and plans for more dockage along the Madison Barracks waterfront. Numerous large yachts are moored in the harbor, whose owners come from throughout central and northern New York. Clearly, a very wealthy population segment repeatedly passes through Sackets Harbor in the summer, and, with the exception of the marinas, local businesses are not really catering to this crowd. Since the harbor is right next to Main Street, visitors from docked pleasure craft should be a potential market for specialized tourist shops. Although there is much room for improve-

Fig. 19   Main Street, Sackets Harbor. The battlefield is at the distant end of this street. Some older structures have been decorated attractively, while others are in poor condition. The impression is of a nice but ordinary Upstate New York village. (Photo by Douglas McDonald)

Fig. 20 Madison Barracks, Sackets Harbor. Historic stone structures like this one would be renovated in the Jobco plan. The spacious grounds of this former army post with its many old buildings makes it easy for visitors to visualize northern frontier military life during the early nineteenth century. (Photo by Douglas McDonald)

ment in the village landscape, entrepreneurs should avoid the over-boutiqued look. Sackets Harbor Village should aim at developing that serenity that belongs to historic places that are maintained for their antique texture and their atmosphere of a bygone era, while fostering appropriately regulated commercial and educational activity.

Madison Barracks
The barracks pose a unique opportunity and a large challenge to developers. Historically they were an essential part of the village. Removal of an active army presence in the 1940s left

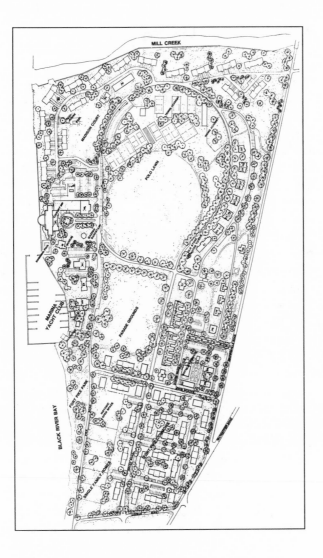

Fig. 21 Madison Barracks Development Plan. Jobco's
plan for Madison Barracks utilizes the existing layout of
this former army base. Shoreline tourist and visitor
facilities anticipate development of a local recreation
industry. Permanent housing areas combine
rehabilitation of former army structures with new
construction. Open space at the parade and polo grounds
is essential to preserve the atmosphere of this historic
site. (St. Lawrence—Eastern Ontario Commission)

the village with no idea of how to recover. The size of the barracks, one hundred acres with approximately a hundred buildings, is particularly daunting. Revitalization of the barracks will require massive infusions of capital. This is not the kind of project that could be sponsored by a few local business leaders.

Nevertheless, Madison Barracks constitutes an unparalleled historic resource for development purposes (Fig. 20). How many villages can boast of such a place? The old stone buildings where U.S. Grant once lived, officers row, the parade grounds, and the larger waterfront structures massively radiate an atmosphere of solid historic nationalism. A visitor conjures up mental images of bands playing, army families engaged in work and play, and taps echoing clearly across the waters of Black River Bay. The very size of the barracks, in contrast to the battlefield, excludes the possibility of inharmonious outside influences.

The development of Madison Barracks must be carefully choreographed so as not to shatter the naturally unified image of that historic landscape. The Jobco plan, a result of negotiation between that group and local authorities, seems to be a step in the right direction (Fig. 21). Jobco's concept calls for developing a residential complex containing everything from single-family homes to mass housing to vacation and commercial facilities. A conference center, museum, marina, riding and tennis academies are proposed. Jobco has agreed to preserve the large open fields in the middle of the complex. If this plan is carried to fruition an infusion of capital and people to Sackets Harbor would bring substantial economic benefits.

Conclusion

In the early days of Augsbury's ownership of Madison Barracks, a consulting firm was hired to advise on the development of the entire Urban Cultural Park area. This firm, Quadrant, Ltd., produced a report that urges a holistic view of preservation for Sackets Harbor (1978). While aimed at the development of a tourist market, the report emphasizes the importance of creating a spatially unified area which will have a heightened impact on visitors. In the words of the report:

> All three elements [battlefield, village, barracks] should be brought together, identified with a common logo or symbol, given a common look in costume, sign treatment and printed material and operated under the same standards and policies. The entire Historic District should be considered a single experience by the traveler and its impact on him must confirm that experience. We must create a saleable travel product under a single name.

If one can look beyond marketing gimmicks, logos, etc., the specific recommendations of this report address movement and experience in space. Sackets Harbor's equivalent of Colonial Parkway, now tentatively called "Harbor Walk," would be a battlefield-to-barracks pathway. Landscaped and with an eye toward providing scenic views of the harbor, the pathway would inform through signs, entertain through festival-like activities, and sell through shops along Main Street. Again in the words of the report:

> All of this must be executed in a coordinated visible fashion so that the visitor senses a dramatic, colorful atmosphere and a lesson in history. He or she must be interested, involved and entertained by the entire experience. It may grate against the principles of the purist and the scholar but great restorations like Williamsburg and Louisbourg are show business. To be successful they must be planned, embellished and executed to interest and entertain—learning education and cultural impact are the results.

The report admits that to accomplish all its recommendations would be a tremendous challenge. In the mid-1980s there are few philanthropic or federal dollars to support such projects. Sackets Harbor must incorporate the ideas and investments of a broad range of public and private sources in its preservation program. "While the concept is uncomplicated, its execution is not. This is a complex project and will require

Fig. 22 Sacket House Visitors Center. Located on Market Square, this historic home was to be the "core" of visitor experience in the historic district. The possibilities for restoration of the structure and grounds have been impeded by the home's being converted to a medical clinic. (Photo by author)

dedicated leadership, corporate and community goodwill, and strong uninhibited cooperation between government, community and the private sector."

Sackets Harbor faces the same conceptual problem with space faced by Colonial National Historical Park, that is, three separate landscapes which, if linked together, could convey a more powerful symbolic image and support a better historic landscape interpretation program. The difference is one of scale. Where fifteen miles separate the sites in Virginia, the three sections of Sackets Harbor are all contained within a one-mile radius.

Proximity, however, does not solve the problem of unification. In fact, to date, Colonial has been more successful in integrating its historic resources than Sackets Harbor. The solution lies in achieving agreement and commitment among relevant leaders. In the case of Colonial, the leaders were of national stature and they managed to carry the project forward in spite of some local opposition. In upstate New York villages, however, the significant leader may be the fire chief or the person on the next stool at the diner.

A recent incident in Sackets Harbor is illustrative of problems faced when working with local leaders. In the period between 1982 and 1984, substantial effort in terms of time and money was directed toward restoration of the Augustus Sacket House. The house was built by the founder of the village and served as a hospital during the War of 1812. It is set back from the harbor on a large lawn between Main and Washington streets (Fig. 22). The Sacket House sits on one side of Market Square, a central location for the entire historic district. A focal feature of the Sackets Harbor Management Plan is to open a visitors center in the house. In the words of the plan, "Sackets House Visitor Center is defined as the core of the visitor's interpretive experience" (SLEOC 1985, one-6).

A visit to the Sacket House during the summer of 1987 revealed no visitor center. This historic, restored building had been remodeled for a Watertown hospital clinic. This totally incompatible use of the Sacket House will set back implementation of the plan and is an example of problems with lack of compromise encountered at local levels. The greatest plan in the world is worthless without informed leadership.

One hopeful trend for Sackets Harbor preservation is demographic. With economic resurgence in the North Country and prospects that more people will want to move to the village and the barracks, the local power structure cannot remain static. In such an environment support should increase for progressive development as outlined in the *Village of Sackets Harbor Urban Cultural Management Plan* (SLEOC 1985).

The historic landscapes of Sackets Harbor still have some impact on visitors in the 1980s. The battlefield is interesting and informative if not inspiring, and the shoreline is spectacular. The village is typical of an older, less prosperous rural America: nice old houses and tree-lined streets with people going about their lives creating a pleasant, slow-paced environment. Madison Barracks still speaks of activity that once stood behind the integrity of a new nation-state. Time has not eroded the meaning and potential of Sackets Harbor landscapes. Still, it will take patience, leadership vision and considerable investment to make Sackets Harbor's historic landscapes models for local landscape preservation.

7. Gettysburg, Pennsylvania

Gettysburg has had the dual distinction of possessing one of the world's great historic landscapes and witnessing one of the greatest historic landscape management fiascos. In the former category is the battlefield pronounced immortal by Lincoln and in the latter the so-called National Battlefield Tower. Fortunately, the latter does not overwhelm the former. Yet the very presence of the tower, with its negative influence on our experience of the landscape, mandates an attempt to understand how such a thing could have happened to one of our nation's most cherished places.

The battle at Gettysburg certainly had great military and political significance. Yet, the battlefield's meaning as a symbolic place for Americans goes far beyond martial perspectives and the battle site's status as a relic. Gettysburg may be viewed as the focal point of two great conflicting causes as well as a memorial to national reconciliation and individual dignity. The spot acquired this meaning not only during a few days in 1863 but also in the years that followed. Today Gettysburg is nationally recognized as a historic landscape with broad symbolic appeal.

Meanwhile, because of the attractive power of symbolic identification, Gettysburg has become a center of recreational activity. Public demands on this small Pennsylvania community are overwhelming. Although the "wheatfield" still grows wheat and cornstalks stand where Pickett's men charged, a commercial strip and tract housing press on the edge of the battlefield. In spite of Gettysburg's national prominence, the 125 years of efforts at preservation and management of its landscape, and the 3800 acres of land in federal ownership, these historic fields are not secure. This is not surprising, for conditions always change at any place, and landscape management must be prepared to deal with that change. The question is whether Gettysburg is adequately prepared in terms of plans and land-use regulations to meet landscape preservation challenges of the late twentieth century.

Local Historical Geography

Most books begin the story of the battle at Gettysburg with a review of the salient features of the town's location. Explaining that Gettysburg was simply a small, southern Pennsylvania market town, narratives of the battle frequently suggest that military action occurred here because many roads from surrounding areas converged on the town. It is true that Gettysburg functioned as a central place in the mid-nineteenth century; that is, it was a place where people came from surrounding areas to sell produce, buy goods, and find services. However, the same could be said of many similar places in the region (Klein 1963). Market towns with radial surrounding route patterns were common.

Gettysburg was, in fact, a somewhat isolated market town. Although the area was part of the seventeenth-century grant to William Penn, settlement began in the east and slowly spread westward, and the land around Gettysburg was not settled until the later half of the following century. The region around Gettysburg backs up to the ridge and valley section of the Appalachian Mountains, and was some of the last land settled on the rolling plains of southern Pennsylvania.

By the beginning of the nineteenth century country roads radiated from Gettysburg toward larger urban places like Philadelphia, Harrisburg, Washington, and Baltimore. Adams County was organized in 1800 and Gettysburg was designated its county seat in 1806. The county contains 526 square miles and is subdivided into townships, one of which, Cumberland Township, surrounds Gettysburg Borough. The multinational English, German, and Scotch-Irish settlers created a small, mixed farming agricultural economy in the area. The landscape surrounding Gettysburg during the summer of 1863 was divided into small, dispersed farmsteads (Fig. 23). Rougher terrain was wooded, while the valleys were heavily farmed. Wooden fences and rock walls divided the fields, and houses and farm buildings were spread throughout the countryside. In 1863 Gettysburg Borough had 2400 residents living in 1050 houses. Any battle fought in this area would inevitably involve civilian lands and lives.

During the summer of 1863 the American Civil War was moving toward a turning point (Catton 1974). Southern resources of men and materiel wore down as battles were fought almost exclusively on Southern soil. An earlier attempt to move the military action to the North had ended in a Southern defeat at Antietam in Maryland. Another Confederate northward thrust was to come. Southern victory in a Northern state not only promised to boost morale, but also might bring about changes in the federal government, turn the tide in border states like Maryland, make Washington insecure, and perhaps increase foreign support for the South.

The federal Army of the Potomac, with an overwhelming manpower advantage, had shown itself incapable of mounting a sustained offensive campaign. As Robert E. Lee and his Army of Northern Virginia moved to the northeast through the ridge and valley section, George G. Meade, the new Union commander, was ordered to keep between Lee and Washington. Lee's choice of a gap eastward out of the ridge and valley section would determine the battle site as the Army of the Potomac paralleled his movements. Temporary plans were made by Union commanders for various defensive positions along this route. They originally thought that the battle would again be in Mary-

Fig. 23   Gettysburg Battlefield, July 1863. Produced around the turn of the
century, this map shows agricultural patterns just before the battle. Dispersed
farms had many small fields for grains and pasture. Cleared valley areas
contrast with forested Cemetery Ridge running south from the borough.
Fences of stone and wood that divided these many fields were appropriated by
the armies for field defenses. Thirty-three historic farms with fifty structures
from the time of the battle are within the park. Only 23 percent of the
1863-era fencing remains. (Gettysburg National Military Park)

land along Little Pipe Creek to the south of Gettysburg. However, Lee continued northeast and left the mountains in southern Pennsylvania heading east toward Harrisburg. No single road was followed by such large forces. Advance Confederate troops encountered Union soldiers on the western outskirts of Gettysburg on July 1, 1863, and drove them back toward Cemetery Ridge south of the borough. Both armies then began to converge on Gettysburg.

The remaining two days of battle saw a titanic effort by the Confederate Army, operating from positions along Seminary Ridge, to push Union troops from their defensive line along Cemetery Ridge. The battle was a classic in military geography involving, on the Confederate side, extended supply and intelligence lines, flanking movements, and a final frontal assault. From the Union standpoint Gettysburg called for concentration of supplies, troops, and fire power in defensive positions ready to react to attack.

The Confederate forces, fewer in number, spread out in a long arc around Cemetery Ridge and, with poor intelligence, mounted gallant attacks that were barely beaten off. The first attack took place around Devil's Den at the left end of Union lines. It was stopped by a desperate movement of Union reinforcements to Little Round Top. Some military scholars consider this to have been the decisive action of the battle. The second, a circling movement through the town and behind the Union center, was defeated by poor timing and quick Union reaction. On the final day General James Longstreet's army corp led an assault, popularly called Pickett's Charge, that was a full-scale attack on the Union center and which resulted in decimation of Confederate forces.

Lee's troops withdrew toward Chambersburg and the South. Many military strategists, including the most famous of all Gettysburg residents, General Dwight Eisenhower, believe that the Army of the Potomac's hesitation in following Lee lengthened the war. Never again did a Confederate army move into a Northern state. The point of farthest advance by Longstreet's troops on the final day of the battle is called the "high water mark of the Confederacy." In a military context the Battle of Gettysburg was a momentous event, and over the years Gettysburg has acquired an even broader meaning for many Americans. Soon Gettysburg had "hallowed" grounds on it hands, and landscape-management problems were an inevitable result.

The borough of Gettysburg was faced with a practical problem in battlefield management immediately following the battle (Davis 1983). More than six thousand bodies lay scattered over various parts of the Battlefield. Arrangements had to be made to bury the dead as soon as possible. At first soldiers and volunteers from the town went on the battlefield and dug shallow graves wherever men lay. Rudimentary identification was written on wooden boards. This was not a permanent solution, however, for these initial graves were shallow and subject to exposure by the elements and agricultural activities. In addition, the North demanded a dignified final resting place for Union dead. Governor Andrew Curtin of Pennsylvania visited Gettysburg immediately following the battle. He authorized expenditure of state funds to acquire land for a Union cemetery. This action brought a Gettysburg lawyer, David McConaughy, into the picture. He was president of Evergreen Cemetery, the private graveyard from which Cemetery Ridge draws its name. Eventually the state purchased additional acreage next to Evergreen Cemetery for military burials. By 1872 the War Department had taken title to the Gettysburg Cemetery as it had with cemeteries at other Civil War sites.

Creation of a national cemetery proved to be an easier task than dealing with the rest of the battlefield. McConaughy had a vision that was much larger than that of merely making adequate provision for the dead. Immediately after the battle visitors came to Gettysburg to view the site of the hostilities, and it was obvious that many more would follow. McConaughy felt that the battlefield would be a fitting memorial to those who had fallen. He shared these ideas with fellow businessmen in the community and set about acquiring battlefield land. Even as Lincoln came to dedicate the cemetery on November 19, 1863, property was being purchased on the battlefield. Since the battlefield covered much of the land around three sides of the town, it was composed of relatively small agricultural holdings. Buying up these properties was not an easy task. Even today, 125 years later, the process of purchasing land is not complete.

In 1864 the Gettysburg Battlefield Memorial Association was chartered by Pennsylvania with McConaughy as its legal counsel. The purpose of this group was to buy battlefield land, build memorials, and lay out roads. Their stated goal was to preserve the battlefield and erect the memorials "to commemorate the heroic deeds, the struggles, and the triumphs of the brave defenders." Thus, this landscape of war was already seen as a reminder of something more than military victory, though only from the Union perspective at that time.

Although the state of Pennsylvania made a small appropriation to the Association, funds for battlefield preservation were slow to accumulate. On the fifteenth anniversary of the battle the Pennsylvania division of a Union veteran's organization known as the Grand Army of the Republic held a reunion at Gettysburg. Soon GAR organizations from all over the country were raising money to finance memorials to various units that had been on the field. The GAR, through its financial contributions to the Battlefield Association, assumed control of the battlefield. By 1895 the Association owned five hundred acres and had erected three hundred memorials.

Support for establishment of a national military park at Gettysburg came from a former Union Corp Commander. General Daniel Sickles, a member of Congress in the 1890s, urged federal ownership of the battlefield in Congress and introduced legislation which led to creation of the park. That law established planning requirements for development of the battlefield, including specific identification of significant land that should be acquired by the federal government. Importantly, the legislation suggested purchasing land adjacent to the battle-field to preserve the appearance of battle sites. This concept of landscape management, which takes into account the lands lying beyond the site of a particular historic event, is important for historic landscape preservation.

When the War Department took over at Gettysburg in 1895, enough time had passed to heal many of the emotional wounds of the Civil War. Prior to this time most efforts to preserve the battlefield at Gettysburg had concentrated on Union positions. The War Department's commission to study acquisition of Battlefield Association lands included a former Confederate general among its members. Henceforth, land was acquired and memorials erected on the entire battlefield, and the inter-pretive program was not to be prejudicial to either side of the conflict. Thus, what had been a major site of battle carnage would be preserved to honor sacrifices of men from North and South. The symbolic meaning of Gettysburg was growing.

Three reunions of Gettysburg veterans have been held on the battlefield. The twenty-fifth, held in 1888, included only Union veterans. However, creation of the National Battlefield, together with friendly contacts among surviving Confederate and Union commanders, led to planning for a grand fiftieth re-union in 1913. Fifty-five thousand veterans from North and South arrived for the festivities. Events included talks, tours, exhibits, opportunities for conversation among old adversaries, and a speech by President Woodrow Wilson. A seventy-fifth re-union was attended by almost 2000 veterans in 1938 and in-cluded dedication of a peace memorial as well as a speech by President Franklin Roosevelt. These gatherings, with atten-dant publicity, heightened public recognition of the battlefield as a memorial to people and ideals, rather than conflict.

By 1933 when the battlefield was turned over to the Na-tional Park Service, the War Department had completed major improvements. Of utmost importance, over 2000 acres of land were then within park boundaries. Today the park includes 3800 acres on which are 1380 memorials, monuments and

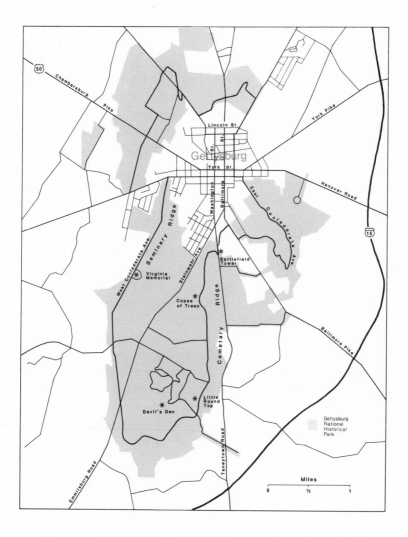

Fig. 24 Gettysburg National Military Park. The national battlefield
surrounds most of the borough, but does not include all battle sites.
The famous radial road pattern is evident. Union positions were
centered on Cemetery Ridge, with Confederates attacking toward
the west, north and northeast from positions on Seminary Ridge.
(Cartography Lab., Dept. of Geography, Univ. of Florida)

markers of various sorts (Fig. 24). In addition, the park contains all or part of 33 farms from the 1860s and about 50 period farm buildings. The land is still crossed by historic defense works and contains archeological artifacts. The Park Service has extensive facilities, including a library and artifact collections.

The present population of the borough is approximately 7000 living in 2225 residential structures (Gettysburg National Military Park 1982). Considerable population growth occurred as Gettysburg changed from an agricultural county seat to a small city with a large-scale tourist industry. Between 1.5 and 2 million visitors tour the park each year.

Factors Affecting the Landscapes of Gettysburg

Gettysburg stands out, even among a host of other special places, and it has attracted considerable attention. Some of that attention has been directed toward the development of commercial enterprises whose viability is based on their proximity to the park. Other people have jealously attempted the preservation and improvement of the historic landscapes. The interaction between these groups and individuals has a long history.

Gettysburg's historic landscapes are associated with a pivotal turning point in the most traumatic period of our nation's history and with the articulation of national purpose by our most revered president. As images of the Civil War and Abraham Lincoln developed over the years, the image of Gettysburg changed as well.

Lincoln: Man and Message
Somewhat surprisingly in a nation of historical as well as geographical illiterates, the Civil War remains an event of profound meaning in popular imagination. Perhaps people remember because that conflict is associated with universally recognized sectional divisions. Or perhaps the personalities of its historic actors have kept it in memory: Robert E. Lee,

Stonewall Jackson, and U. S. Grant are still well known today. Looming above all, as the embodiment of the ideals of the prevailing side, is Abraham Lincoln.

Lincoln's commanding position in American history is based on interpretations of his life: his humble origins like those of the common man, his achievement in rising to the presidency, and his sacrifice on the altar of an ideal (Warner 1958, 272). The Gettysburg Address linked the man to the place in an interactive process, with Lincoln lending his prestige to the landscapes and the battlefield giving him a setting of great prominence (Nevins 1964). The culmination of this symbolism of person and place is found in the Gettysburg Address. The reality of war, so terribly expressed in battle and suffering, was given meaning for a nation through the words of a martyr-to-be. That the actual mood at the speech was less than solemn, the delivery and reception poor, and the President convinced that the speech had not gone well; all have some basis in fact. It matters little that some of the details of the occasion don't match the image.

In the text, Lincoln answered a question that was uppermost in public consciousness (Dos Pasos 1964). Perhaps it is the one question that everyone asks at one time or another: Is there some eternal meaning to human events and lives? Particularly when the human scene appears incapable of rendering justification, almost everyone looks for some metaphysical assurance that the human struggle is not in vain. The Civil War must have brought that universal question to the forefront of public attention, and the Gettysburg Address provided an answer.

Above all there was an inspirational purity in Lincoln's Gettysburg Address. People know that to be human is to corrupt experience with motives and desires that are less than honorable. The Civil War in the North was replete with leaders who served themselves better than their country. Lincoln's moral superiority "was due to the depth and weight of his religious sense of the meaning of the drama of history, and his consequent sensitivity to the problem of the taint of self-interest in the definitions of meaning, by which human agents corrupt the meaning in which they are involved" (Niebuhr 1964, 86). In the address, Lincoln gave purpose and dignity to the sacrifices of the common soldier in a message that eventually would come to have meaning for South and North. The site of the address is one of the most frequently visited at Gettysburg. And although Lincoln came from the Midwest, he is forever associated with the landscapes of a small town in southern Pennsylvania.

But what of that place? Can it retain enough of the aura of 1863 to companion the historic landscapes, or are changes that must inevitably occur going to be of such magnitude that they will dim our vision of Gettysburg?

Boundaries and Historic Landscapes
Historic landscapes are seldom islands of tranquility, sitting by themselves in isolated splendor. More frequently, while reminding us of important messages from the past, they exist as constituent parts of a modern world. As integral units of a functioning environment, historic landscapes have to be nurtured. This nurturing is not an attempt to stop development beyond historic landscape boundaries, but to find compromise regulations that will meet all needs.

The federal government through the Department of Housing and Urban Development funded a project in the early 1970s to explore possibilities of planning for growth at Gettysburg. The result of this project was a report which defined three jurisdictions in the immediate park area (National Park, Gettysburg Borough, and Cumberland Township) as "communities" with interrelated concerns (Wallace et al. 1972). This call for cooperative planning and regulation went unheeded.

Several years later a report by the Federal Advisory Council on Historic Preservation suggested that townships beyond Gettysburg Borough seem to have little interest in preserving the larger context of the Park (1976). The council noted that since most land in the town is developed, pressure will increase to develop areas outside the immediate borough. Recommendations included a familiar call for a combination of local, state, and federal regulatory actions to protect the historic landscapes of the Gettysburg region.

Gettysburg National Military Park recognizes the importance to its mission of landscape preservation within and outside the park. Questions of landscape heritage and preservation are addressed at numerous places in the latest "General Management Plan," a document that sets guidelines for operation of the Park.

> The visual setting . . . is the park's most important environmental feature: the visual experience at Gettysburg gives meaning to the events that took place there. . . . This historical landscape gives visual meaning to all of the park's themes and sub-themes. It consists of numerous factors in addition to the all important natural and topographical features including the cultural features of historic roads and lanes, the farmsteads, fields, orchards, woodlots and fencing. (Gettysburg National Military Park 1982, 8, 35)

In addition, the plan indicates accepted approaches to land use control as it affects surrounding landscapes.

> The communities surrounding the park have undertaken, to various degrees, efforts to plan for and to control land use and regulate growth. The Park Service, in general, encourages neighboring communities to take actions to control land use to protect local interests which also consider Federal interests. Zoning provides for all the needed land uses in a community, while guiding their location and where appropriate minimizing impacts on neighboring properties. The types of controls that will complement the park's historical lands include the establishment of agricultural and historic districts, clustered development, screening, height restrictions and other actions to minimize visibility of development in sensitive areas. (11)

In spite of universal recognition by professionals that regional planning is needed, the park's neighboring jurisdictions have moved with glacial slowness toward land-use controls. Many local residents seem unaware of any landscape-context concept and think of the park and park concerns as being confined to its actual physical boundaries. Thus, park "territory" is a much smaller area for many park neighbors than it is for landscape preservationists (Altman and Chemers 1980, 135).

Local reluctance to initiate protective regulations for areas visible from the park has led a congressional committee to question the suitability of the park's current boundaries. The battle and associated events took place on virtually all areas surrounding the borough. Enabling legislation for creation of the park in 1895 authorized acquisition of acreage that approximates current holdings. No one has ever anticipated that the federal government would take title to all Gettysburg battle sites. On the other hand, the present 3800 acres is not sufficient to protect the visual scene. The Park Service would probably be satisfied with adequate land-use controls in neighboring areas, without acquiring more land. However, a possibility that the federal government may need to intervene, under its mandate to conserve historic resource for all people, has led to the current study.

Battlefield Interpretation

Most places explain themselves. Interpretation is individual for ordinary landscapes because viewers have different backgrounds, and when we visit unfamiliar places we orient ourselves by reference to previous experience in similar settings. If we go to a farm our experience is influenced by what we already know of agricultural landscapes. Landscape meaning is passively conveyed and is taken in by the spectator through observation and assimilation. In contrast, active interpretation explains places. When landscapes are identified as special places, they are likely to be given some form of active interpretation. Such interpretive programs involve creating signs, exhibits, theatrical presentations, literature and, most intimately, promoting interaction with informed individuals. Public funds may be expended to present historic landscapes to the public. Private enterprise sometimes sponsors interpretation in association with their businesses, which may include actual ownership of historic sites like Fort Ticonderoga and or recreational "attractions" in association with them.

Good interpretation provides visitors with a high-quality experience of the place. With a combination of National Park Service Programs, plus private interpretive activities, visitors are faced with a wide array of choices. This aspect of battlefield interpretation at Gettysburg has its dangers since there is relatively little quality control over private operations. The so-called Lincoln Train Museum has a loudspeaker system blaring honky-tonk music across the Park Visitors Center grounds—audible pollution. The home of the only civilian casualty of the battle is dominated by a gift shop. The *New York Times*, reporting on Gettysburg during the summer of 1986 in conjunction with a rededication ceremony at the Pennsylvania memorial, suggested that an unfortunately large number of visitors experience the battlefield landscape through various private museums and air-conditioned buses (Serrin 1986).

Of particular concern in this regard has been the long history of private tour guides. From earliest post-battle days, local residents conducted tours of the battlefield. Charles Hosmer got some reaction to this situation at Gettysburg in his interview with Verne Chatelain, former chief historian of the Park Service. In response to Hosmer's suggestion that during the 1920s there was a feeling among preservationists that historic areas would speak for themselves, and therefore, needed little interpretation, Chatelain said:

> Yes. And of course for many years the War Department had been entrusted with the National Battlefield sites, as in places like Gettysburg where the tourist interest was naturally very high; but the opportunity to get a reasonably credible, accurate story with all

the devices that would make for a clear understanding of what happened there was simply lacking. A national program simply didn't
exist. There was the atrocious system at Gettysburg; there still is
to some extent, but it's been softened a great deal over the years—
the atrocious system of commercial guides who develop their own
ideas of what they should say to the tourists who came in. And also
their own ideas of what they should charge them. The visitor often
had very disagreeable experiences in some of those areas. (Hosmer
interview)

The War Department began a system of testing and licensing
tour guides around 1915. This program to promote skilled interpretation has continued under the National Park Service. A
1987 survey suggests a relatively high degree of satisfaction
with licensed guides at Gettysburg (Machlis and Baldwin, 46).

In recent years I've learned that my own family had personal
contact with the early interpretive program at Gettysburg. My
maternal grandfather was thoroughly enamored with Gettysburg. He was very active in private enterprise in this country
and abroad and had been since his youth. Having had no time
for formal education he was self-taught, familiar with the clas-
sics of Western civilization (often carrying a copy of Plato in
his pocket), and a thoughtful observer of his native land. He
was convinced that a visit to Gettysburg was essential to an
understanding of this country and urged such a visit on my
newlywed parents around 1927.

They made an all-day trip from New York by car. My mother
recalls driving into the town and hiring an individual guide
from among a number who were standing around. To the considerable chagrin of my grandparents, the visit was not a success. It was not until we visited the battlefield as a family
many years later that my mother felt she received an adequate
orientation. Of course, one cannot generalize about Gettysburg
interpretation on the basis of a single family's experience.
Nevertheless, it is interesting to note that my parents' two
visits spanned the period when battlefield control changed

and the Park Service developed an interpretive program at Gettysburg.

As with most other historic landscapes in the country, Gettysburg is predominantly oriented toward interpreting an event. By this I mean that programs are directed toward explanation of what occurred on the landscape, rather than of the setting itself. This site was a small mixed farming region before arrival of contesting armies. Field patterns, structures, fences, and roads of Gettysburg were typical of a relatively prosperous middle Atlantic agricultural area. Armed conflict on a massive scale severely disrupted normal landscape patterns and the lives of inhabitants. A complete interpretation of this historic landscape, including an exploration of nineteenth-century rural life as well as of the battle experience of soldiers and citizens, would be extremely worthwhile. Gettysburg National Military Park has made some tentative efforts along these lines with one of the old farmsteads.

The Tower at Gettysburg

In the 1890s those in charge of the evolution of Gettysburg's landscape faced a fateful decision. For several decades a trolley offering battlefield tours had been in operation. The trolley ran along tracks laid in a circular route through the heart of the battlefield. When the federal government took possession of the park, legal action was initiated to condemn these tracks. On January 27, 1896, a federal court upheld condemnation proceedings with a decision that read in part:

> The importance of the issue involved in the context of which this great battle was a part cannot be over-emphasized. The existence of the government itself and the perpetuity of our institutions depended upon the result. . . . Can it be that the government is without power to preserve the land and properly mark out the various sites upon which this struggle took place? Can it not erect the monuments provided for by these Acts of Congress, or even take possession of the field of battle in the name and for the benefit of

all citizens of the country for the present and for the future? Such a use seems necessarily not only a public use, but to be within the powers granted by Congress. (160 U.S. 668 1896, 681–82)

The decision stated that there was a Constitutional basis for preservation of the battlefield because of its importance to our national heritage. This precedent established at Gettysburg was invoked in other places in years to come.

The battlefield at Gettysburg is almost ideally suited for panoramic viewing from a number of locations. Union lines were stationary along Cemetery Ridge, and Confederate assaults came from parallel Seminary Ridge, so it is not difficult to obtain visual perspective from a number of natural, elevated positions. Visitors to Gettysburg today can hardly help noticing a gigantic steel structure on the crest of Cemetery Ridge. Designed to provide a view of every spot on the battlefield, it can also be seen from every location in the park. Ironically, at the place that witnessed a precedent-setting condemnation aimed at preserving a historic landscape, authorities were unable to prevent construction of the prototypical scenic monstrosity in America, the 1970s-era Battlefield Tower.

The Gettysburg Battlefield has had more than one tower. Around the turn of the century, the War Department commission that ran the park had five steel towers built at various locations. These early towers were used in military training. Although they were unnatural features of the landscape, they did not significantly intrude because of their relatively small size. Those towers are of the walk-up variety and in the range of sixty to seventy-five feet tall (Fig. 25).

The rationale behind erecting a tower in excess of three hundred feet, completely out of scale with every other feature of the landscape, can best be understood in light of Gettysburg's development as a tourist center following World War II. Adams County had remained a relatively isolated, if prosperous, mixed farming region before that time. No major cities were close enough for commuting, and transportation to the area was de-

Fig. 25   War Department Tower. These towers, erected around the turn of the century, were used to study military tactics. Five original towers, of which three remain, stood from sixty to seventy-five feet tall. These towers match the scale of surrounding vegetation. (Photo by author)

pendent on cars. The growth of automobile culture in the postwar years opened a tourist boom. Gettysburg visitors, who before had never reached a yearly total of a million, would exceed 2 million per year in the space of a few decades.

Tourists attract those wishing to provide services for travelers, and the necessity for overnight accommodations and restaurants in the area became obvious. However, along with those necessities other establishments arose that fall under the general heading of "attractions." So-called museums of many varieties and shops peddling memorabilia all vie with one another through architectural and signatory excess. In the words of William C. Davis, "Commercial development, dependent upon the Battlefield for its lifeblood, was actually threatening destruction of much of the scenic impact" (1983, 41).

In 1970 a private businessman, Thomas R. Ottenstein, informed the National Park Service that he was forming a corporation to build a three-hundred-foot observation tower in the borough of Gettysburg near the intersection of Steinwehr Avenue and Baltimore Street (Oyler 1972). Ottenstein used Park Service estimates of 8 to 10 million visitors by 1980 to project huge profits for his tower and amusement tax income for the community. These projections have proved to be totally inaccurate. More than a poor business decision, erection of the tower is a denial of everyone's Constitutional rights to preservation of a historic landscape important to our nation's heritage.

The only reason that such a structure could be built near the park was that the borough of Gettysburg and Cumberland Township lacked effective land-use control through zoning. This laissez-faire approach to development, combined with the lure of increased tax dollars from an outside entrepreneur, convinced many local citizens to support the tower. Local leaders were divided on the tower along fairly traditional conservative-liberal lines. Relations between different groups in the community were not warm. The liberal, environmentalist side drew support from the local park personnel and Gettysburg College.

The conservative, developer viewpoint garnered strength from business and controlled the borough council. When local politicians were unwilling to oppose the tower, national leaders soon took notice. The director of the National Park Service and noted environmentalists across the country recognized the threat at Gettysburg. As a result of publicity and maneuvering by those involved in the controversy, Ottenstein moved the site of the tower to a point next to the Pickett's Charge field off Steinwehr Avenue. However, this location was even worse from a preservation standpoint because of its proximity to the park. Both sides prepared for legal confrontation.

The story from this point on might best be described as a comic opera if the consequences had not been so tragic. A lawyer for the environmentalists was given access to Park Service records but then switched sides because those opposed to the tower were not able to meet his demands for a retainer. Thus, he was able to provide inside information to Ottenstein interests. The Park Service in Washington, without consultation with its local personnel, concluded that legal opposition to the tower was unlikely to succeed. A political appointee of the Service negotiated a settlement with Ottenstein that gave access across Park Service land to a site on Cemetery Ridge. That action removed the federal government from the case. State and local environmental interests remained in opposition to the tower. The Commonwealth of Pennsylvania used their own legal staff to try the case. In such a complex and important case this was a questionable decision. Thus, an issue vital to the preservation of one of our nation's most important historic landscapes was contested by unequal teams of lawyers and decided by a local Adams County Court Judge.

The Commonwealth submitted expert testimony opposed to construction of the tower. For example:

It is my opinion that the construction of a 300-foot tower near or in Gettysburg National Military Park is a long step in the process of cheapening and commercializing the battlefield area. The battle-

Fig. 26   The Modern Tower. This tower looms over monuments along Cemetery Ridge. Its size is not appropriate for this landscape, and the structure disturbs visual experience. (Photo by author)

field is an historic site which means a great deal to the people of Pennsylvania and the United States. A tower of this size and of such proximity to the Park will detract from the historic meaning of this area. (Affidavit of Bruce Catton, July 15, 1971, Commonwealth v. National Gettysburg Battlefield Tower)

And:

Such a tower would be visible from every position on the battlefield, and would continually spoil a visitor's efforts to reconstruct in his imagination the events that occurred in 1863. We today are stewards for future generations and as such we owe it to them to conserve this beautiful and historic site unimpaired. We would be irresponsible stewards if we did not put a prompt halt to the planned construction. (Affidavit of Stewart Udall, July 16, 1971, Commonwealth v. NGBT)

In an unbelievably uninformed decision that suggests how shortsighted local leaders can be, Adams County Judge John A. MacPhail stated that the Commonwealth failed to show that "natural, historic, scenic and aesthetic values of the Gettysburg area would be permanently harmed" by the tower (Opinion of Court, 10/26/71, 15–16). The judge said that arguments about the tower being out of scale with the rest of the landscape were too subjective, that Gettysburg was already highly commercialized, and that the Park Service agreement with Ottenstein implied federal approval of the plan (Oyler 1972, 279–81). Subsequent appeals to federal courts were denied, and the tower was opened in 1974—fitting testimony to judicial and administrative folly (Fig. 26).

Surveys of Gettysburg Visitors
A key test of the success of historic landscapes is the kind of experience they provide their visitors. This kind of experience is very hard to gauge, however, because of its complex, subjective nature. In part, site characteristics—including structural appearance, signs, exhibits, programs, and assisting personnel—influence visitors. But the personal traits of the visitors

themselves, as well as the expectations they bring to the landscape, must also be taken into consideration.

Programs and funding that support development and maintenance of historic resources at Gettysburg, as at other places, tend to be cyclic in nature—and stronger at some times than others. In recent years there have been some obvious reasons for this varying level of support. In the late 1950s and early 1960s considerable effort was made by the National Park Service to spruce up Civil War Parks for the Civil War Centennial. Following that time, the attention and fiscal resources of the Park Service turned toward the bicentennial of America's Revolutionary War. Many observers of Gettysburg suspect that a spurt of preservation interest at the park and in town during the late 1970s was in reaction to the tower crisis. Partially in shame for what had happened and in a desire to see that nothing of that kind occurred again, officials in the Park Service and the surrounding political units renewed efforts to protect their scenic environment.

During this later period the Eastern National Park and Monument Association, a non-profit organization associated with the Park Service at numerous sites, commissioned a visitors' survey at Gettysburg (Barnes 1979). This survey, conducted by scholars from Pennsylvania State University, was based on 2,800 five-page questionnaires distributed at various Gettysburg locations on randomly selected dates. The mail return on the survey was 596, or 21 percent. Hypotheses of the study were based on market segmentation theory, which holds that consumers can be classified according to desired outcomes from a market experience. In this case, the market is Gettysburg and the desired outcomes are the visitors' expectations of experiences in the park.

Principal findings of the survey were derived from answers to questions that sought to identify the most influential factors in people's decisions to visit Gettysburg. Analysis of the findings segmented reasons for visiting into four categories: education (to develop knowledge, to appreciate heritage), authenticity (to have a genuine experience, to avoid commercialism), tranquility (to rest, to enjoy the natural landscape) and action (to do a lot of things). While the survey does not specifically address questions of what a landscape experience entails beyond mere enjoyment of the scene, there are suggestive hints in each response category concerning visitors' expectations of the environment at places like Gettysburg.

Approximately 80 percent of the respondents came to Gettysburg with expectations that might be logically associated with such a place—that is they hoped to find education, authenticity, and tranquility. People in these three categories participate in different park activities, depending on their specific category. Those seeking education spend more time at the National Park and Cemetery and do not visit many outside attractions. Those seeking authenticity do more on their own and avoid packaged tours. The tranquility group seems to associate that quality with less strenuous, group-oriented activities.

The action group, and a smaller group of individuals who seem to have little place-specific motivation to visit Gettysburg, exhibit different behavior patterns. On the questionnaire, action was equated with doing a lot of things. Thus, predictably, members of this group attend some of the attractions and are heavier users of the tower. These are younger visitors, and seem to think of Gettysburg as being just another tourist destination.

A more recent survey at Gettysburg was conducted by the Cooperative Park Studies Unit at the University of Idaho (Machlis and Baldwin 1987). Visitors to eleven different sites in the park during the week of July 22, 1986, were randomly selected to participate in the survey. One thousand ninety-three surveys were handed out, of which 454 were returned for a response rate of 41 percent.

The survey instrument is a small booklet, self-addressed and stamped on the back. Its main section is a map upon which a single member of a visiting group is asked to indicate the sites he or she visited in chronological order. Next, respondents are to indicate what the group did from a list of generalized activities (motorized travel, picnicking, hiking, viewing museums, etc.) during various two-hour periods of the day. The remainder of the survey includes standard questions about the visiting group, and about specific activities at the park. A final question states: "One of the goals of Gettysburg National Military Park is to maintain the battlefield in a pre-battle appearance and the Eisenhower Farm in a 1951–1969 appearance. While you were visiting the park, were you distracted by modern buildings or structures?" Respondents are invited to answer this question with more than a yes or no if they wish.

Results of the survey indicated that most visitors came in small groups and were from all over the country. Heaviest visitation was during the middle of the day, and about half stayed overnight in the area. The most popular sites were the Visitors Center, National Cemetery, and Little Round Top, with over 80 percent going to those spots. Most visitors expressed satisfaction with their visit.

One survey question asked visitors if they viewed the draft of the Gettysburg Address or visited the site where Lincoln spoke. Eighty-six percent had done one or the other, with 52 percent having done both. Only 14 percent of visitors to the park had no exposure to the Gettysburg Address. It requires a special effort to see the draft or visit the site of the Address, as both are located at places other than the Visitors Center. Thus, Lincoln's continued importance to the Gettysburg Park message is proven by these figures.

Of particular interest to this study are responses to the "distracted by modern structures" question. Local Park Service personnel were invited to suggest specific questions for the survey, and, clearly, this question was formulated with the tower in mind, although it was not mentioned specifically. Twenty-five percent of respondents indicated that they had been distracted by modern structures. A review of individual survey forms shows that an overwhelming majority of these respondents refer to the tower when they use the write-in section. The following were popular phrases for describing the tower: "stupid," "a travesty," "an abomination," "out of place," "detracts and distracts," "a disgrace," "inappropriate," "obtrusive," "horrible," ungainly," and, the most popular, "an eyesore." These responses prove beyond a doubt that the tower has "permanently harmed" historic landscapes at Gettysburg.

In my own visits to Gettysburg and other historic landscapes I have been impressed with the general good taste and serious attitude displayed by most citizen-visitors. It is quite moving to observe visitors when they approach the draft of the Gettysburg Address in a vault at the Cyclorama. In general people move slowly and speak quietly. Parents explain to children, sometimes incorrectly but with obvious reverence, circumstances surrounding the Address. While there will always be some exceptions, we can be proud of the American public who visit historic landscapes.

Thus, while a wide variety of people travel to a place like Gettysburg, a significant number of those going to a site with well-known historic association seem to be seeking an educational and emotional experience. Landscape planners and managers can count on an interested and in some ways demanding public. This is just one of the reasons for seeking to preserve, protect, and enhance historic landscape resources while limiting those human activities that would interfere with appropriate public utilization.

Historic Landscapes of Gettysburg

Without doubt the most important factor accounting for the preservation of Gettysburg landscapes has been 125 years of land acquisition, first by private individuals, then by the Battlefield Association, and since 1895 by various departments of the federal government. Thus, while population and tourist growth has placed pressure on the available land, a countervailing force has acted to restrain incompatible land development. This informal approach to preserving the landscape has simply worked out over the years without legal control. Resulting landscapes range from relatively pristine scenes to commercial strips. However, the decade of the 1970s proved that Gettysburg can no longer depend on an informal system to maintain its historic landscapes and that legal controls have become essential.

Steinwehr Avenue

Steinwehr Avenue begins as a southwesterly fork off Baltimore Street, the main north-south thoroughfare in Gettysburg. It runs directly through the battlefield between Cemetery and Seminary Ridges and across the field of Pickett's Charge as the Emmitsburg Road. It was along this road that Robert E. Lee originally planned to attack Union positions on Cemetery Ridge (Fig. 27). The roadbed was a strategic position during the battle, and it occupies a strategic position in present struggles to develop landscape management for Gettysburg.

Steinwehr Avenue is the most direct connection between the borough and the National Military Park main entrance. It is not surprising that over the years, with virtually no zoning controls to inhibit incompatible use, a commercial strip has developed there (Fig. 28). With the exception of an ordinance that has served to tone down obnoxious signs, Steinwehr Avenue today looks like many small-town commercial strips. It is a two-lane street, congested with traffic during heavy park visitation periods, and lined with a variety of food, lodging, and entertainment establishments. The congestion hampers the efficiency of services to the public.

Steinwehr Avenue is so close to the edge of the park that it detracts from the atmosphere of that place. Visitors standing on Cemetery Ridge see not only the field across which twelve thousand Confederates attacked in 1863 but also the arches through which latter-day Americans streamed to consume uncounted billions of hamburgers. Steinwehr Avenue assaults contemporary senses with a vast, offensive display of commercialism. The Advisory Council on Historic Preservation, in its 1977 report on Gettysburg, suggests short- and long-range strategies to deal with Steinwehr Avenue. For the immediate future the report proposes a structural decoration ordinance to control building color and landscaping requirements. Long-range solutions require a different approach. The report says: "In the case of Steinwehr Avenue, the ideal would be to phase out strip development and replace it with more compatible land uses" (6).

A late 1970s-era master plan for Gettysburg National Military Park called for creation of a new entrance and visitors center northwest of Gettysburg. This plan would do away with inappropriate uses of Cemetery Ridge and provide needed services with less adverse effect on battlefield landscapes. The Advisory Council advocates acquisition of enough land to provide an appropriate setting for the commercial establishments that would be displaced from Steinwehr Avenue. Thus, it is a restoration plan for this historic street, and it represents a major conceptual advance in landscape preservation. However, Pennsylvania's failure to provide funding for a necessary highway bypass has indefinitely shelved the plans for a new visitors center and the accompanying relocation of business.

Little Round Top

At Gettysburg, July 2, 1863, was a day dominated by Confederate attempts to turn both ends of the Union line along Cemetery Ridge. At the southern end of the ridge Union forces averted disaster by a very narrow margin. One Union Corp commander in the area was General Dan Sickles, known in later years as the major mover behind efforts to get federal control over Gettysburg's battlefield. Sickles advanced his corp, in a controversial movement, from Cemetery Ridge to an exposed site

Fig. 27 Baltimore Street and Emmitsburg Road, 1860s. Emmitsburg Road (Steinwehr Avenue today) forks to the right off Baltimore Street. Today a convenience store occupies the site of the house in the fork of the road. The twin-chimneyed house in the left background now has two-story columns in front and serves as an attraction called "A. Lincoln's Place." The side-gabled houses on spacious lots stretching in the distance down Emmittsburg Road contrast strikingly with the commercial strip located here in the 1980s. (National Park Service)

Fig. 28 Emmitsburg Road (Steinwehr Avenue), 1980s. This photograph was taken approximately 3 thousand feet from the fork with Baltimore Street. The national park entrance is at the left. The other side of Steinwehr Ave. is occupied by "attractions," motels, restaurants, and gas stations. The golden arches of a famous restaurant chain can be seen on the horizon. Pickett's Charge field is just over the hill. Steinwehr Avenue is dominated by commercial activity which disturbs views from a number of important positions along Cemetery Ridge. (Photo by author)

Fig. 29   Electric Railroad Trolley Track, 1890s. The trolley ran along a
railbed in the valley between Little Round Top in the background and Devil's
Den. This was a scene of some of the heaviest fighting on the second day of
the battle. The trolley line was condemned as a desecration of the battlefield.
(Gettysburg National Military Park)

near the Emmitsburg Road. Confederate forces led by General
Longstreet attacked this position with great success. Sickles'
corp was destroyed as a fighting force, which opened the way
for Confederates to gain a position at the south end of Cemetery Ridge on a hill known as Little Round Top.

The strategic importance of Little Round Top was based on
the fact that its high ground overlooked all Union lines to the
north. If Confederate artillery were mounted on Little Round
Top, it would be within range of the most important Union
positions. In addition, Confederate control of Little Round Top

Fig. 30 Trolley Track Site, 1980s. Monuments on the top of Little Round Top and in the left foreground near Devil's Den provide orientation to the scene. Ninety years later it is hard to argue that removal of rails and substitution of road traffic has improved this scene. Widespread discontent with current conditions has led the Park Service to plan for removal of all transportation facilities from this valley. (Photo by author)

would open movement to the rear of Union positions. At the last possible moment, independent action by several Union officers, who took it upon themselves to move troops from other locations to defend the high ground while waiting for arrival of reinforcements, saved Union control of the hill.

The trolley line condemned in 1896 passed below Little Round Top in the valley next to Devil's Den. A comparison of photographs taken at approximately the same spot near Devil's Den looking toward Little Round Top suggests that if concern in 1896 was for preserving battlefield character, similar concern is justified today when tour buses, modern roads, and parking facilities threaten the scene (Figs. 29 and 30).

The Park Service has been considering possible solutions and is experiencing the difficulties encountered in corrective efforts with most historic landscapes. The general goal in this case is to get all modern activity out of Little Round Top's view. The current management plan (Gettysburg National Military Park [GNMP] 1982) suggests elimination of modern roads, and rerouting of traffic along portions of the old trolley bed to a less visible side of the valley. Further study, proposals, public hearings, and reflection have resulted in a plan to completely eliminate traffic from the immediate valley area (GNMP 1986). In the future, traffic movement will be rerouted throughout the park in conformity with the chronological events of the battle. Little Round Top area traffic will go along the back of Cemetery Ridge and around to the back of Houck's Ridge (Devil's Den), where visitors will walk to the valley rim to look in either direction. Special facilities will be constructed for handicapped access to the scene. All of these changes, the detailed and extensive study as well as a projected cost of approximately one million dollars, are due to admirable National Park Service attempts to protect these historic landscapes.

During the early years of War Department control, an effort was made to clear land and plant trees in patterns similar to those existing in 1863. This vegetative-control program continues today. Gettysburg's *General Management Plan* estimates that three hundred more acres of woods exist within the park than at the time of the battle (1982, 33). There is a program to eliminate some of this non-historic woodland. Historic agricultural land in the park is farmed through a special permit program. Since corn today looks as it did 125 years ago, visitors see an agrarian landscape that approximates that found by Confederate and Union forces on July 1, 1863.

At Gettysburg particular attention is paid to preserving

boulders. These large rocks served as protection during the battle and are used as reference points for comparing old photographs with modern locations. Vegetative-control programs expose the mid-nineteenth-century boulder-strewn landscape. Thus, the look of the land is not identical to, but certainly suggestive of, the look in 1863.

Visitors to Little Round Top see a vast historic landscape quite similar to that seen by Union defenders of 1863 (Fig. 31). The western slope of the hill is steep and strewn with boulders. On the other side of a small stream at the foot of the hill, at a distance of several hundred yards, is Devil's Den. The large boulders are a popular picnic and children's play area. Beyond are fields leading to the Emmitsburg Road and the Eisenhower Farm National Historic Site. On the horizon are mountains that were the source of and the escape route for Lee's Army of Northern Virginia.

To the north of Little Round Top is the lower section of Cemetery Ridge, the field of Pickett's Charge and Gettysburg Borough (Fig. 32). Larger monuments are visible on parts of the battlefield. Little Round Top's view includes most sites of battle action and is thus particularly useful for understanding the military action. Although paved roads and motor vehicles are visible, the panorama is predominantly pastoral. The historic agrarian nature of this landscape invites the spectator to imagine a time before the conflict when farm families experienced everyday lives far from the center of their nation's attention. In that sense, Little Round Top is a tranquil, introspective spot on the battlefield and is certainly one of the great historic landscape vistas in the United States.

The Virginia Memorial
For many years after the battle, few markers of any sort were found along former Confederate lines on Seminary Ridge. A number of factors were responsible for this situation. First, it took some time for emotional feelings associated with the

Fig. 31 Devil's Den. This area of large boulders is located across a small stream at the bottom of the slope. A determined Confederate attack up this hill on July 2, 1863, almost turned the tide of the battle. Roads visible in the valley are scheduled to be removed. (Photo by author)

Fig. 32 Little Round Top Observation Area. This view toward the north shows the potentially commanding position this site could have been for Confederate forces. The Pennsylvania Memorial is seen in the center on Cemetery Ridge, while the Battlefield Tower intrudes on the right side of the picture. The borough of Gettysburg is on the horizon. The scene is slightly more wooded than in 1863. (Photo by author)

Civil War to decline to reasonable levels. Then, too, the battle-ground was in the North and represented a significant loss for Confederate forces. After the war former Confederate states returned their dead to the South, and neither veterans organizations nor states from that region participated in marking the field that was then managed by a Union veterans group.

By the time the federal government took over at Gettysburg there was a desire on the part of many leaders in the North and South to rectify this inequity. The commission established to oversee battlefield land holdings had Southern representation

Fig. 33 Virginia Memorial. The field of Pickett's Charge stretches toward the horizon. The famous copse of trees, focal point of attack, is just above the left edge of the memorial. That constant irritant, the tower, is seen to the left. (Photo by author)

and made significant efforts to acquire land along Confederate lines. Attempts were made to mark Confederate positions. However, another obstacle stood in the way of erecting Southern monuments. Rules governing erection of markers stated that the memorials should be placed along battle lines. For Union forces this was no problem since they had been relatively stationary on Cemetery Ridge throughout the battle. In the case of Southern forces, however, their battle lines had been along Seminary Ridge, but they fought in front of Union lines, a considerable distance away. Thus, only two markers from Southern organizations were erected by the turn of the century.

The fiftieth reunion in 1913 was a great healer of emotional wounds. Southern monuments were clearly appropriate for the battlefield, and the stalemate over Southern participation in monument development was broken with Virginia's Memorial in 1917. That memorial, with Robert E. Lee astride Traveller on top and troops gathering for action at the bottom, commands one of the great sites on the battlefield (Fig. 33). It was from this point that Lee ordered Longstreet to launch Pickett's Charge. Cemetery Ridge rises in the background with its copse of trees, focal point of the attack. One can imagine a massive surge of troops and understand the awesome task of facing artillery on the ridge across the valley. The visual scene so clearly conveys the magnitude of the power opposing Lee that the consequent horrors of shattered and destroyed lives are easily imagined and one feels a tremendous sense of loss.

Into this landscape, filled with symbolic meaning and emotion, intrudes a gigantic structural pillar. Looming just behind Cemetery Ridge is the Battlefield Tower, discordant with the historic landscape, and representing contemporary values that pale to insignificance in relation to what occurred here during the Civil War. Like the mindless graffiti that imposes itself upon us in so many public places, the tower is an obscenity on the landscape.

Conclusion

A civil war is a national trauma—even more than a foreign war. In conflicts between nations there is generally less national introspection. Feelings of nationalism engendered by foreign wars cloud vision and block interchange among disparate peoples coming to grips with their destiny. This is not to suggest that individual emotional experience is untouched by foreign war but that such a conflict can often be experienced by a nation without leading its citizens to examine the fundamental assumptions of their nationhood. At least that seemed to be the case with us before Vietnam.

Military cemeteries on foreign soil seem curiously remote. Emotionally it would be better if soldiers were buried back home. The removal of Confederate bodies from Gettysburg was a natural response to this kind of emotion. Southerners were, after all, trying to establish a separate country. But in the context of our nation's history, it would have been better if their graves had remained in Pennsylvania. The healing of our nation would have been quickened by Northern and Southern burials in the Cemetery at Gettysburg. Historic landscapes have that kind of power.

J. B. Jackson writes of Gettysburg as a place dedicated to the common soldier. He notes a change in the character of Gettysburg's battlefield monuments. "One reason for this change was that the American public no longer thought in terms of heroes, of the generals who had commanded the two armies as the only individuals deserving to be honored. There were tens of thousands of soldiers, many of them volunteers, who had fought and died and deserved a collective monument" (1980, 94). It is at places like Gettysburg that people come to commune with and appreciate fellow citizens of 125 years ago; one nation of the people, across the ages, coming together. The preservation of historic landscapes at such a place contributes something essential to this experience. The landscapes of Gettysburg fulfill a basic human need.

In community-power terms, Gettysburg has had a long and checkered landscape-preservation history. Leaders during the Civil War responded to demands for a place dedicated to Union soldiers. Government provided a cemetery and private interests began acquisition of the battlefield. In the more than a hundred years since the war, government intervention has increased in support of Gettysburg landscape preservation. Federal take over of the battlefield was an initial step in a process that continues today. The isolated failures at Gettysburg, such as the tower, have sprung from unwarranted exercise of power by local economic interests. From the perspective of a landscape-preservation belief system, failure at Gettysburg has been due to an inability to successfully articulate collective property rights and governmental responsibilities on the basis of Constitutional principles.

Protection of landscapes like Gettysburg is costly. This cost is not only in dollars but also in limitations on personal choice. Just as national interests prevailed in the Civil War, so national property rights must be judged supreme at Gettysburg today. At one time at Gettysburg, as substantial a piece of private entrepreneurial property as a railroad was condemned and removed. This action was taken to preserve the integrity of the battlefield's landscape. There must come a time when the tower, that blatant incongruity, receives similar treatment and is destroyed.

8. Managing Historic Landscapes

This book began by defining landscape as a mental construct, "a composite image of space." We do well to remember this primacy of the mental image when we prepare to manage landscapes. What is really there on the ground is less important than what people think is there. A distracting feature, for example, may occupy only a very small percentage of the field of view, but if it dominates our thinking its actual size is irrelevant.

The landscapes studied in this book were categorized as "historic," meaning that they have a symbolic and emotional meaning for significant numbers of Americans and are associated with an event or era of the past. It was then suggested that an attempt to understand how these places have evolved over time could be systematized by reference to community power, particularly to the concept of a historic landscape belief system. This system was defined very broadly to include everything from beliefs based on fundamental Constitutional principles to compromise solutions for specific landscape problems. Four historic landscape sites were studied to illustrate typical problems that arise as people attempt to develop and preserve places that register strongly in human consciousness.

I believe that this study has posed and answered some questions that repeatedly challenge those of us who are concerned about, and sometimes acquire power over, landscapes. These questions and their answers will serve as a conclusion.

Why should historic landscapes be preserved?
The importance of historic landscapes to an understanding of national identity can hardly be overemphasized. Landscape forms and patterns evolve over time and are based on the fundamental methods and beliefs of a culture. Meinig writes that landscapes "arise out of deep cultural processes as a society adapts to new environments, technologies, and opportunities and as it reformulates its basic concepts related to family, community, and the good life" (1979, 184).

Historic landscapes give observers a chance to commune with their formative past. The message of each historic landscape is a communication about the values of a culture. Landscape patterns develop through time and reveal something of the challenges and accomplishments of other eras. The realization that each of those settlers at St. Augustine and Jamestown, as well as the soldiers at Gettysburg and Sackets Harbor experienced these landscapes, and that to a degree we can share those experiences, prompts us to consider what characteristics of landscape meaning are constant across the ages. We partake of the same spatial experiences our forebears underwent as they searched for national identity.

Historic landscapes have the potential to stimulate some of us to be better citizens: to think about, write about, vote or act concerning issues of national significance—such as war and peace, human rights, the environment, etc. Recognizing the importance of historic landscape appreciation to an understanding of nationhood prompts spectators to undertake the "reading" of those places. Methods used to probe landscapes are limited only by the scope of imagination, and the ensuing messages landscapes give off are diverse. While the general nature of the message of a special place may be shared, there are also an infinite variety of individual interpretations. A knowledge of place history, the use of all our senses, reference to scholarly analysis and literary works, and individual contemplation are all useful tools for experiencing particular historic landscapes.

Historic landscapes are composite images of space shared by many people. The fact that these special landscapes are widely recognized as important places makes them particularly revealing of contemporary culture. Our notions of landscapes derive from an anthropocentric perspective, that is, people experiencing the land as revolving around and taking meaning from human activities. This is a universal experience. Special places provide an added dimension to human experience. If the ordinary landscapes of everyday life seem impermanent and confusing, extraordinary landscapes conveying grand messages comfort us with the realization that noble values endure and that we are not alone in the human struggle. St. Augustine, Colonial, Sackets Harbor, and Gettysburg are exceptional landscapes, but not necessarily monuments to exceptional people. They speak of nation-founding and of people like us facing and solving problems in the passage of events and time.

What does community power tell us
about landscapes?
Landscapes don't develop in a societal vacuum. Their constant change is controlled, sometimes tightly and other times in a random fashion. Control is the effect of power, usually a power based on some kind of belief system, while randomness suggests anarchy.

Community power theorists are divided into two camps, elitists and pluralists. The major area of contention between these theories concerns identifying and determining the characteristics of people in power. Elitism contends that leaders are drawn from those with shared economic interests, often property at the local level, and that they act in consort because of these interests. Pluralists claim that, through democratic processes, leaders represent different interest groups and compete among themselves to control action. Some community power studies suggest that there are many types of power structures in communities, ranging from strict elitism to democratic pluralism. Most local communities possess power structures that scapes to preserve characteristics of an era in the past. Even when landscape preservation is focused on a particular time period, change is unavoidable—and probably desirable.

Preservation chooses to stabilize certain landscape elements and not others. Judging what to preserve is not easy, and well-preserved landscapes of today may be considered poorly preserved in the future. Preservation values that most often change are those concerned with methods of interpretation: what should be explained and how should it be done? Williamsburg, for example, is viewed quite differently within the preservation community today from the way it was sixty years ago. Preservation there has remained an attempt to convey the truth. But definitions of what constitutes Williamsburg truth and how it should be interpreted have been questioned.

Structural surveys from St. Augustine's early preservation efforts reveal that little remains from the Spanish Colonial period. Over the years, and in spite of efforts by many dedicated individuals, the historic district has had difficulty establishing its credentials for authenticity. Lack of leadership vision has allowed incompatible commercial activities near genuine historic sites. Were it not for the Castillo, under National Park Service control and lending its aura of truth to the rest of the scene, St. Augustine would not be a significant historic landscape.

It is necessary to have facilities like motels and restaurants near historic sites. "Attractions" that claim to entertain spring up along roads surrounding special places, and these figurative weeds along historic paths may have some useful function. Yet, amid the clutter, it must be remembered that the raison d'être is the historic landscape. Good interpretation is difficult to achieve when historic sites are smothered by commercialism. The best possible interpretation of historic landscapes will provide better returns, economic as well as emotional, for all citizens.

Sometimes it is necessary to correct the mistakes that have been made in the past with historic landscapes or with their interpretation. Removing offensive landscape elements or rethat the battle was not conducted in isolation. The first day of fighting included a large-scale Union retreat through the borough toward Cemetery Ridge. Townspeople hid Union men who were cut off by that retreat, and the town supplied civilian volunteers for the battle and for the cleanup afterward. The approach, departure, and supply of the troops occurred over numerous routes in the region. In spite of these considerations, the importance of Gettysburg Borough and the surrounding region are not effectively interpreted at Gettysburg.

The management plan at Sackets Harbor calls for overall economic development that will make the village, battlefield, and barracks viable entities within an integrated historic district. Landscape development would attract new residents and visitors, thus compounding economic growth. This is an extremely ambitious plan designed to do more than just interpret a historic landscape for tourists. The historic military importance of the site and its natural environment are the points suggested for emphasis in the overall plan for Sackets Harbor interpretation. The state battlefield wants to emphasize navy life in the nineteenth century through four different interpretive areas. If these plans were expanded to include an interpretation of army life at the barracks and civilian life in the village, Sackets Harbor could be a showplace of early nineteenth-century Americana.

The best hope for effective landscape preservation and interpretation at Sackets Harbor Battlefield is to concentrate on military action in the War of 1812. This could be approached in the same manner as at Gettysburg. The point is not to glorify war but to ask visitors to ponder larger questions naturally associated with armed conflicts. At Gettysburg these were national unity, individual liberty, and personal sacrifice. At Sackets Harbor they might well be the more specific issues of how the frontier was defended and the gains of the American Revolution consolidated and preserved. Sackets Harbor is challenged to improve battlefield interpretation and link its separate sites through a single, cohesive theme.

*Why are military action sites attractive
to Americans?*

Historic landscapes chosen for this study have widely varying characteristics. They have dissimilar settings, have acquired meaning during different historic eras, faced different kinds of challenges to development, and are under varied forms of control. It is probably not surprising, since human history exhibits all too often the cyclic return to armed conflict, that all these places witnessed military action at some period. St. Augustine was the scene of several raids, although it does not emphasize this aspect of its history to visitors. The Yorktown Battlefield is part of Colonial, and Sackets Harbor Battlefield is adjacent to that village. Of course, Gettysburg is dominated by the battle.

In comparison to citizens of other developed countries, Americans seem unusually interested in battlefields. In particular, battle sites associated with major turning points of our national drama attract attention. Revolutionary War and Civil War battlefields stand out especially. Is it that fortress America has been able to mentally isolate armed conflict, assigning meaning to events in a seemingly less complex, less interrelated area of the world? Do interpretations of our relatively short period of national independence tend to emphasize momentous events? Do distinct American educational, entertainment, communications, or belief systems stimulate the attraction of martial places? I hope our predilection for battlefields is not a sign of a national "six-gun" mentality. Fortunately, battlefield preservation has not excluded protection for other types of historic landscapes in the United States; the preservation movement is testimony to that.

It becomes apparent when studying such places that a battle can serve as a powerful symbolic focus for historic landscapes. For some people a battle represents the strength and pride of nationhood. Since American sites tend to highlight American military victories, a battlefield can represent an ultimate win. This is, of course, one of the reasons that Gettysburg was not as popular among southerners. To others a battle site calls for deeper insight. The fact that conflict is past and peace restored prompts some to ask whether it was worth it, whether the conflicting principles were important enough to justify loss of life. Historical perspective almost always suggests that the battle could have been avoided in the search for resolution of disagreements. Hence, although battle sites may be visited by those who revel in the imagined glories of military action, such places may also serve as inspiration for renewed dedication to peace.

There seems to be nothing quite so potent for lending symbolic meaning to a landscape as the associations it conjures up of people who made the ultimate sacrifice for an ideal. It matters little how ill-conceived were the strategies, tactics, or execution of battle action, nor whether the ideal was noble. Giving one's life for an ideal is a powerful image that sanctifies ground where sacrifice took place.

Gettysburg is, of course, the epitome of such a place. For those with regional loyalties the battle calls up many associations. Principles such as individual dignity, national unity, states' rights, and dedication to a cause are represented on that field. Beyond those, Gettysburg was clearly a site of one of the major turning points of our national experience. Yorktown was longer ago, involved a foreign rather than brotherly enemy, and seems to evoke less emotional reaction than Gettysburg. Nevertheless, it is clearly recognized as a battle site of first-rate significance.

The War of 1812 is relatively unknown in this country. Some people know of military action in Maryland and around the capital, but few are familiar with circumstances on a "northern frontier." There are striking contrasts in interpretation of the War of 1812 on different sides of the United States–Canadian border. Loyalist military activity is the focal point of a number of historic places in Canada. Sackets Harbor could be an American counterpart, and even a linkage to, those Canadian places. To accomplish this, fuller interpretation of the period and the place must be available to the visitor.

*What is government's role in landscape
preservation?*
Many historic parks in the Northeast are threatened by urban
sprawl (Shabecoff 1987). The Manassas Civil War Battlefield in
Virginia, at the southern end of Megalopolis, is a prime example of this threat. A shopping mall and housing area were
planned for a section of that battlefield outside, but visible
from, the park. Preservationist protests led to federal purchase
of the site. Antietam is often cited as a similar case, and we
have reviewed the problems of uncontrolled development at
Gettysburg. The most effective way of responding to these
threats and upholding the rights of Americans to retain their
historic landscapes is through government action. These actions could include, but are not limited to, buying additional
land for preservation, buying historic easements that require
private owners to retain the historic character of property, and
enforcing zoning restrictions. Federal funding to support these
actions is bound to be severely limited in the future.

Preservation leadership should come from both the private
and public sectors. Public officials bring a needed perspective
to preservation. Some government professionals are trained
and experienced at responding to landscape preservation challenges. Government land-use regulations are best met with
government help, and public historic landscapes should be controlled by public servants. Landscape preservation is such a
complicated task that many places use the skills of a wide
range of specially trained professionals. Those that Hosmer
called "carpetbagger preservationists" in the 1930s at St. Augustine were needed then, and are even more necessary today.
Small communities seldom have the personnel resources to
provide for professional attention to landscape preservation. It
is left to government at the state level and above to supply consultants for such tasks. Local residents could not have put together the management plan required at Sackets Harbor. The
St. Lawrence Eastern Ontario commission of New York State
provided professional assistance.

Of course, the prime agency for this professionalism nation-wide has been the National Park Service. Naturalists in the Park Service were vital for protection of western scenic parks. Arrival of the Park Service in the East and acquisition of historic parks brought professional historians, architects, archeologists and others to the service of historic landscapes. Unfortunately, the Reagan administration of the 1980s has had a decidedly regressive view of the role of government in landscape preservation. Department of Interior budgets were slashed, scenic parks were opened to exploitation by resource industries, land acquisition programs were eliminated, and hiring was severely curtailed. Colonial National Historical Park, containing buried artifacts on Jamestown Island and elsewhere, does not have an archeologist on its staff. Gettysburg, with a history of traffic congestion and strained community relations, doesn't have a permanent planner. The result of budget cuts has been understaffing, career stagnation and morale problems in the Park Service.

Historic landscape preservation faces problems that are unique to our age. These challenges call for some redefinition of governments role in the preservation movement. Consider the problem of the automobile and facilities for its use. Roads and parking lots have become a ubiquitous presence on American landscapes. Yet, cars are not authentic features of most historic landscapes. Government has the primary responsibility for regulating mass movement around historic landscapes. This is an awesome charge since there are documented cases of historic resource damage caused by ill-advised transportation schemes. The routing of traffic toward the Plaza and near the Castillo at St. Augustine is definitely a hindrance to historic interpretation there. Colonial has provided for travel between sites by automobile, whereas Williamsburg forbids cars in the historic district. One of the main features planned for linking sites at Sackets Harbor is a "pathway" that does not exclude cars. Gettysburg Park authorities propose rerouting of non-historic routes across the battlefield. Every historic landscape must contend in some way with the automobile problem.

A standard approach is to make the automobile as inconspicuous as possible while providing alternative forms of transportation. Vegetative screening of parking lots, strategic placement of roads, walled-off historic areas, and attractive walkways are approaches that have been tried at various sites. Of course, large numbers of people are not natural features of most historic landscapes either. Because we have an anthropocentric view of landscapes, excess human presence may not seem as objectionable as too many cars.

In one way the automobile can be successfully utilized in conjunction with historic landscapes. That is, the car provides for individual contemplation of historic places. Crowded buses and packaged comments from tour guides may detract from efforts of individuals to fully experience a historic landscape. Thus, attempting to make automobiles inconspicuous while using them to provide opportunity for individual contemplation of the scene is a delicate, but desirable goal. Planning for such action requires using professional advice and securing government approval.

Nobody challenges the legitimate role of private enterprise in landscape development. But, from a community power perspective, government has a vital and legitimate role in landscape preservation as well. Through compromise public and private interests combine to protect our landscape heritage. The Constitutional right of citizens to high-quality landscape experiences implicitly involves government in the landscape-preservation movement.

Can we form a national historic landscape preservation ethic?

Justification to protect and manage historic landscape resources is based on a belief that these places educate and stimulate the kinds of creative reflections that are good for people and critical for the nation. It is unfortunate that we are a nation of historic and geographic illiterates. Mention of history and geography means nothing beyond the memorization of a handful of dates and place names to most Americans. What people lack in knowledge and schooling can be partially supplied by personal association with historic landscapes. Historic landscapes performing this vital function don't interpret themselves, and more attention needs to be given to the educational aspects of landscape preservation. It should be remembered that interpretation must be enjoyable as well as informative. Even relatively uneducated persons are attracted by entertaining presentations at historic sites, and they soak up informative interpretive programs like a dry sponge. The sight of roads converging on a town, of colonial streetscapes, pioneer settlement areas, and soldiers' living quarters can—with a little guidance to viewers—effectively convey information about historic and spatial relationships. People often have to experience historic landscapes to link the affective with the cognitive, to really think about people in time and space and not just memorize facts.

Historic landscapes are important to our nation—recreationally, educationally, emotionally. Where are we headed in the future if our citizens can't interpret our past? National Park Service professionals are aware of their responsibilities, but they need better support. One thing this country must have is a strong national policy not only for preserving past landscapes but also for promoting use of these special places for discretionary time activity.

Let's adopt a National Historic Landscape Preservation Ethic, because the presence of these places in the United States is a visible tribute linking a wide range of individual and collective concerns. Historic landscapes represent a happy convergence of interests since they simultaneously reflect individual rights to property and collective rights to quality place experience, while contributing to our understanding of events, people, and places of the past. They are testimony to our national commitment to America's heritage.

Mental images are idiosyncratic. One person stands by the Virginia Memorial at Gettysburg lost in thoughts of rebel yells and massed men under waving flags advancing toward Cemetery Ridge. Another visitor to the same point thinks sadly of the human carnage. A third viewer ponders the ideals contested on July 1–3, 1863, and is silently grateful for the outcome. Another simply enjoys a pleasant pastoral scene. (One of the four is offended by the tower on the horizon.) Gettysburg and other evolving historic landscapes deserve preservation and enhanced interpretation for the sake of these experiences.

Appendix

A. Sense-of-Place Profile

Place location   _____
Observer location   _____
Date and time   _____
Weather conditions   _____

Rate each factor for contribution to the sense of place of rater, using a -3 to +3 range representing very negative to very positive, with irrelevant factors assigned a score of 0. Assign significance value of each factor on a .1 to 1.0 range. Multiply rating by significance. Subtotal scores for site and human characteristics.

	Rating	x	Significance	=	Score
Site characteristics					
Relative location					
Topography					
Water					
Vegetation					
Micro-climate					
Lighting					
Boundaries					
Visibility					_____
Subtotal					
Human characteristics					
Color					
Texture					
Sounds					

(continued on next page)

	Rating	x	Significance	=	Score
Smells					
Paths					
Edges					
Public Facilities					
Blight					
Composition					
Scale					
Activity					
Mystery					
Subtotal					
Total					

B. Compatibility Matrix

Place location _____
Date and time _____
Weather conditions _____

Rate each landscape characteristic for place experience using the following scale: + (high compatibility), * (moderate compatibility), - (low compatibility), 0 - (no compatibility). Pattern of results assists in understanding components of sense of place at any location.

	Place experience		
	Relaxation	Recreation	Education
Landscape Characteristics			
Physical setting			
Structures			
Commercial activity			
Open space			
Historic site			
Markers			
Public Facilities			
Population movement			

Bibliography

Advisory Council on Historic Preservation. 1976. *A Plan to Preserve the Historic Resources of the Gettysburg Area of the Commonwealth of Pennsylvania.* Washington: U.S. Government Printing Office.

Agnew, John, John Mercer, and David Sopher. 1984. *The City in Cultural Context.* Boston: Allen and Unwin.

Albright, Horace M. 1931. Letter to K. Chorley, Jan. 5. National Archives Record Group 79.

Altman, Irwin, and Martin Chemers. 1980. *Culture and Environment.* Monterey, Calif.: Brooks/Cole.

Appleton, Jay. 1975. *The Experience of Landscape.* London: Wiley.

Bachrach, Peter. 1967. *The Theory of Democratic Elitism: A Critique.* Boston: Little, Brown.

Barnes, John D. 1979. *Visitor Use Study: Gettysburg National Military Park.* Eastern National Park and Monument Association.

Bird, James H. 1985. "Geography in Three Worlds: How Poppers Can Help Elucidate Dichotomies and Changes in the Discipline." *Professional Geographer* 37 (4): 403–9.

Blaut, James M. 1984. "Modesty and the Movement." In Thomas F. Saarinen et al., eds. *Environmental Perception and Behavior.* Dept. of Geography, Univ. of Chicago, no. 209, 149–63.

Bolton, Roger. 1987. "An Economic Interpretation of a 'Sense of Place': Speculations and Questions." Paper, Association of American Geographers, Portland, Oregon.

Bowden, Martyn. 1984. "Environmental Perception in Geography: A Commentary." In Thomas F. Saarinen et al., eds. *Environmental Perception and Behavior.* Dept. of Geography, Univ. of Chicago, no. 209, 85–92.

Brown, Ralph H. 1948. *Historical Geography of the United States.* New York: Harcourt, Brace and World.

Brookfield, H. C. 1969. "On the Environment as Perceived." *Progress in Geography* 1:51–80.

Buttimer, Anne. 1983. *The Practice of Geography.* New York: Longmann.

——. 1984. "Perception in Four Keys: A Commentary." In Thomas F. Saarinen et al., eds. *Environmental Perception and Behavior.* Dept. of Geography, Univ. of Chicago, no. 209, 251–63.

Buttimer, Anne, and David Seamon, eds. 1980. *The Human Experience of Space and Place.* London: Croom Helm.

Butzer, Karl W. 1978. *Dimensions of Human Geography.* Dept. of Geography, Univ. of Chicago, no. 186.

Catton, Bruce. 1974. *Gettysburg: The Final Fury.* New York: Doubleday.

Chokar, B. A. 1986. "Development in Environmental Behavior Design Research: A Critical Assessment in the Context of Geography and Planning with Special Reference to the Third World." *Environment and Planning* 18:5–26.

Chorley, Kenneth. 1932. Letter to Albright, July 12. National Archives Record Group 79.

——. 1947. Letter to Judge David Dunham, March 17. Archives of the Colonial Williamsburg Foundation.

——. 1948. Letter to Congressman Bland, June 3. National Archives Record Group 79.

Clay, Grady. 1973. *Closeup: How to Read the American City.* New York: Praeger.

Conzen, M. R. G. 1981. "Historical Townscapes in Britain: A Problem in Applied Geography." In J. W. R. Whitehand, ed. *The Urban Landscape: Historical Development and Management.* New York: Academic, 55–74.

Cook, Ian G. 1974. "The Sense of Place in the Nottingham Derbyshire Coalfield." Paper, Institute of British Geographers, Annual Conference, Norwich.

Cook, R. U., and J. C. Doornkamp. 1974. *Geomorphology in Environmental Management.* Oxford: Clarendon Press.

Cosgrove, Denis E. 1984. *Social Formation and Symbolic Landscape.* Totowa, N.J.: Barnes and Noble.

Costrove, Denis E., and Peter Jackson. 1987. "New Directions in Cultural Geography." *Area* 19 (2): 95–101.

Cotter, John L. 1958. *Archeological Excavation at Jamestown.* Archeological Research Series no. 4, National Park Service. Washington, D.C.: Dept. of the Interior.

Craik, Kenneth H. 1986. "Psychological Reflections on Landscapes." In Edmund Penning-Rowsell and David Lowenthal, eds. *Landscape: Meanings and Values.* London: Allen and Unwin, 48–64.

Crouch, Dora P., Daniel J. Garr, and Axel I. Mundigo. 1982. *Spanish City Planning in North America.* Cambridge: MIT Press.

Dahl, Robert A. 1961. *Who Governs?* New Haven: Yale Univ. Press.
———. 1971. *Polyarchy: Participation and Opposition.* New Haven: Yale Univ. Press.

Datel, Robin E., and Dennis J. Dingemans. 1984. "Environmental Perception, Historic Preservation, and Sense of Place." In Thomas F. Saarinen et al., eds. *Environmental Perception and Behavior.* Dept. of Geography, Univ. of Chicago, no. 209, 131–44.

Davis, Burke. 1982. *The Campaign That Won America.* New York: Eastern Acorn Press.

Davis, J. E. 1928. *Jamestown and her Neighbors on Virginia's Historic Peninsula.* Richmond: Garrett and Massie.

Domhoff, G. William. 1986. "The Growth Machine and the Power Elite." In Robert J. Waste, ed. *Community Power: Directions for Future Research.* Beverly Hills: Sage, 53–75.

Dos Pasos, John. 1964. "Lincoln and His Almost Chosen People." In Nevins, Allan, ed. *Lincoln and the Gettysburg Address.* Urbana: Univ. of Illinois Press, 15–37.

Downs, Roger M. 1970. "Geographic Space Perception." In *Progress in Geography*, vol. 2. London: Edward Arnold, 65–108.

Drury, Newton B. 1937. "Visit to St. Augustine." Report. National Park Service Records, National Archives Record Group 79.
———. 1948. Letter to Congressman Bland, July 19. National Archives Record Group, 79.

Dunbar, Gary S. 1973. "Illustrations of the American Earth." *American Studies* 12 (1): 3–15.

Duncan, James S. 1985. "Individual Action and Political Power: A Structuralist Perspective." In R. J. Johnston, ed. *The Future of Geography.* London: Methuen, 174–89.

Duncan, James S., and Nancy G. 1984. "A Cultural Analysis of Urban Residential Landscapes in North America: the Case of the Anglophile Elite." In John Agnew et al., eds., *The City in Cultural Context*. Boston: Allen and Unwin, 255–76.

Dunkle, John R. 1955. "St. Augustine, Florida: A Study in Historical Geography." Ph.D. diss., Clark University.

Dye, Thomas R. 1986. "Community Power and Public Policy." In Robert J. Waste, ed. *Community Power: Directions for Future Research*. Beverly Hills: Sage, 29–51.

Dye, Thomas R., and L. Harmon Ziegler. 1981. *The Irony of Democracy*. 5th ed. North Scituate, Mass.: Duxbury.

Eiseley, Loren. 1957. "The Enchanted Glass." *American Scholar* 26: 478–92.

Ernest, Gary G. 1986. "The Four Features of the Sackets Harbor Battlefield or Thoughts on a Balanced Exhibit Program." Alexandria Bay, N.Y.: Thousand Island State Park Region.

Fairbanks, Charles H. 1976. "From Missionary to Mestizo: Changing Cultures of Eighteenth-Century St. Augustine." In Samuel Proctor, ed. *Eighteenth-Century Florida and the Caribbean*. Gainesville: Univ. Presses of Florida, 88–99.

Field, G. Lowell, and John Higley. 1980. *Elitism*. London: Routledge and Kegan Paul.

Florida Board of Parks and Historic Memorials. 1958. *St. Augustine Restoration Plan*. Pamphlet.

Ford, Larry R. 1974. "Historic Perspective and the Sense of Place." *Growth and Change* 5 : 33–37.

———. 1984. "Where Do We Go From Here? A Commentary." In Thomas F. Saarinen et al., eds. *Environmental Perception and Behavior*. Dept. of Geography, Univ. of Chicago, no. 209, 145–48.

Forman, Henry Chandlee. 1938. *Jamestown and St. Marys': Buried Cities of Romance*. Baltimore: Johns Hopkins Univ. Press.

Gardner, Malcom. 1934. Memo to Colonial Superintendent, April 3. National Archives Record Group, 79.

Gettysburg National Military Park and National Cemetery. 1982. *General Management Plan* National Park Service. Washington, D.C.: Dept. of the Interior.

Gettysburg National Military Park 1986 *Little Round Top/Devil's Den Development Concept Plan* Washington.: N.P.S. Dept. of Int.

Gibson, Edward. 1978. "Understanding the Subjectivity of Meaning of Places." In David Ley and Marwyn Samuels, eds. *Humanistic Geography: Prospects and Problems*. Chicago: Maaroufa, 138–52.

Glassie, Henry H. 1975. *Folk Housing in Middle Virginia*. Knoxville: Univ. of Tennessee Press.

Golledge, Reginald, and Helen Couclelis. 1984. "Positivist Philosophy and Research on Human Spatial Behavior." In Thomas F. Saarinen et al., eds. *Environmental Perception and Behavior*. Dept. of Geography, Univ. of Chicago, no. 209, 179–90.

Good, Albert H. 1940. "Architectural Report on the Old Town of Yorktown." April 15. Files of Branch of History, Dept. of the Interior. Washington, D.C.: Mimeo.

Goodey, Brian. 1973. *Perception of the Environment*. Birmingham, U.K.: Center for Urban and Regional Studies, no. 17.

———. 1987. "Environmental Perception: The Relationship with Urban Design." *Progress in Human Geography* 11 (1): 126–33.

Gould, Richard A., and Michael B. Schiffer, eds. 1981. *Modern Material Culture: The Archeology of Us*. New York: Academic Press.

Graham, Thomas. 1978. *The Awakening of St. Augustine*. St. Augustine: St. Augustine Historical Society.

Gray, D. E., and S. Greber. 1979. "Future Perspectives." In C. S. Van Dorne, G. B. Priddie, and J. E. Lewis, eds. *Land and Leisure: Concepts and Methods in Outdoor Recreation*. Chicago: Maaroufa, 3–24.

Harrington, J. C. 1939a. Memo on Jamestown status, May 18. Branch of Hist. Dept. of Int.

———. 1939b. Archeological Research on APVA Grounds. Oct. 12. Files of Branch of History, Dept. of the Interior, Washington, D.C. Memorandum.

Hatch, Charles E. 1980. *Colonial Yorktown's Main Street and Military Entrenchments*. New York: Eastern Acorn Research Series.

Hawley, Willis D., and Frederick M. Wirt, eds. 1974. *The Search for Community Power*. Englewood Cliffs: Prentice-Hall.

Holman, M. A. 1961. "A National Time Budget for the Year 2000." *Sociology and Social Research* 46: 17–25.

Hosmer, Charles B., Jr. 1965. *Presence of the Past: A History of the Preservation Movement in the United States Before Williamsburg*. New York: G. P. Putnam.

————. Interviews. Department of History Archives, Principia College, Elsah, Illinois.

    Roy Appleman, April 15, 1970

    Herbert E. Kahler, June 19, 1970

    Albert Manucy, November 11, 1972

    Verne Chatelain, September 17, 1971

————. 1981. *Preservation Comes of Age: From Williamsburg to the National Trust, 1926–1949.* Charlottesville: Univ. of Virginia Press.

Hunter, Floyd. 1953. *Community Power Structure.* Chapel Hill: Univ. of North Carolina Press.

Jackson, John Brinckerhoff. 1980. *The Necessity for Ruins.* Amherst: Univ. of Massachusetts Press.

————. 1984. *Discovering the Vernacular Landscape.* New Haven: Yale Univ. Press.

Jellicoe, Geoffrey, and Susan Jellicoe. 1987. *The Landscape of Man.* London: Thames and Hudson.

Kahler, Herbert E. 1937. Report to National Park Service Director, March 4. National Archives Record Group, 79.

Kelso, William A. 1978. *America's Democratic Theory: Pluralism and its Critics.* Westport, Conn.: Greenwood.

Kinser, William M. 1987. "Cross Creek: Planning for the Development of an Environmentally, Culturally and Historically Sensitive Area." M.A. Thesis, Univ. of Florida.

Klein, Frederic Shriver. 1963. *Just South of Gettysburg: Carroll County, Maryland in the Civil War.* Lancaster, PA.: Wickersham.

Lamme, Ary J. III. 1984. "American Remembrance: Preserving a Rural Heritage." *Christian Science Monitor,* July 16:15.

————. 1989. "Preserving Special Places." *Geographical Review* 79(2): 195–209.

————. 1986. "Seeing Rural America." *Christian Science Monitor,* June 30:18.

Larkin, Robert P., and Gary L. Peters. 1983. *A Dictionary of Concepts in Human Geography.* Westport, Conn.: Greenwood.

Larrabee, Edward McM. 1968. *Sackets Harbor 1967 Excavation Report.* Thousand Islands State Park Commission.

Laurie, Ian C. 1975. "Aesthetic Factors in Visual Evaluation." In Ervin Zube et al. 1975a. *Landscape Assessment: Values, Perceptions, and Resources.* Stroudsburg: Douden, Hutchinson and Ross, 102–17.

Lazer, W. 1982. "A Scenario for the Future—The Next Fifteen Years." In J. B. Fridges and D. J. Allen, eds. *Michigan Tourism: How Can Research Help?* East Lansing: Michigan State University.

Lee, Ronald F. 1946. Memo to National Park Service Director, May 15. National Archives Record Group 79.

Leighly, John. 1958. "John Muir's Image of the West." *Annals of the Association of American Geographers* 48 (4): 309–18.

Leone, Mark P. 1981. "Archeology's Relationship to the Present and the Past." In R. A. Gould and M. B. Schiffer, eds. *Modern Material Culture: The Archeology of Us.* New York: Academic Press, 5–14.

Lewandowski, Susan J. 1984. "The Built Environment and Cultural Symbolism." In John Agnew et al., eds. *The City in Cultural Context.* Boston: Allen and Unwin, 237–54.

Lewis, Peirce. 1975. "The Future of the Past: Our Clouded Vision of Historic Preservation." *Pioneer America* 7 (1): 1–20.

———. 1979. "Axioms for Reading the Landscape." In D. W. Meinig, ed. *The Interpretation of Ordinary Landscapes.* New York: Oxford, 11–32.

Ley, David. 1981. "Behavioral Geography and the Philosophies of Meaning." In Kevin R. Cox and Reginald G. Golledge, eds. *Behavioral Problems in Geography Revisited.* New York: Methuen, 209–30.

———. 1985. "Cultural/Humanistic Geography." *Progress in Human Geography* 9 (3): 415–23.

Lowenthal, David. 1961. "Geography, Experience, and Imagination: Toward a Geographical Epistemology." *Annals of the Association of American Geographers* 51 (3): 241–60.

———. 1966. "The American Way of History." *Columbia University Forum* 9:27–32.

———. 1968. "The American Scene." *Geographical Review* 58 (1): 61–88.

———. 1979. "Age and Artifact: Dilemmas of Appreciation." In D. W. Meinig, ed. *The Interpretation of Ordinary Landscapes.* New York: Oxford, 103–28.

———. 1985. *The Past Is a Foreign Country.* Cambridge: Cambridge Univ. Press.

Lowenthal, David, and Hugh Prince. 1965. "English Landscape Tastes." *Geographical Review* 55 (2): 186–222.

Lynch, Kevin. 1972. *What Time Is this Place?* Cambridge: MIT Press.
———. 1976. *Managing the Sense of a Region.* Cambridge: MIT Press.
MacArthur, John R. 1986. "Give Me Old-Time USA Without the Glass." *Preservation News* 26 (3): 5.
Machlis, Gary E., and Sara B. Baldwin. 1987. *Gettysburg National Military Park.* Visitors Services Project Report No. 7, Cooperative Park Studies Unit, Univ. of Idaho, 3 vols.
Maeder, Richard H. 1986. Letter to author, Nov. 19.
Mahon, John K. 1972. *The War of 1812.* Gainesville: Univ. Presses of Florida.
Marth, D. and M. Marth. 1983. *Florida Almanac.* Gretna, La: Pelican Publishing.
Martin, Peter E. 1984. *Pursuing Innocent Pleasures: The Gardening World of Alexander Pope.* Hamden, Conn.: Archon.
Matthews, M. H. 1984. "Cognitive Mapping Abilities of Young Boys and Girls." *Geography* 69 : 327 – 36.
McCloskey, Robert. 1943. *Homer Price.* New York: Viking.
McGurn, Ken. 1988. "Cross Creek Charity." *The Business Journal* 2, no. 28 (February 25).
Meinig, Donald W. 1971. "Environmental Appreciation: Localities as a Humane Art." *Western Humanities Review* 25 (1): 1 – 11.
———. ed. 1979. *The Interpretation of Ordinary Landscapes.* New York: Oxford.
———. 1986. *The Shaping of America: Atlantic America, 1492 – 1800.* New Haven: Yale Univ. Press.
Mills, C. Wright. 1956. *The Power Elite.* New York: Oxford Univ. Press.
Murgerauer, Robert. 1984. "Mapping the Movement of Geographical Inquiry: A Commentary." In Thomas F. Saarinen et al., eds. *Environmental Perception and Behavior.* Dept. of Geography, Univ. of Chicago, no. 209, 235 – 43.
Murtagh, William G., and G. C. Argan. 1983. "Historic Districts: Identifying Social Aspects of Preservation." In Norman Williams, Jr., et al., eds. *Readings in Historic Preservation.* New Brunswick, N.J.: Center for Urban Policy Research, 130 – 31.
Nairn, Ian. 1965. *The American Landscape.* New York: Random House.
Nelson, J. G., and R. W. Butler. 1974. "Recreation and the Environment." In I. R. Manners and M. W. Mikesell, eds. *Perspective on*

Environment. Washington, D.C.: Association of American Geographers, 290–310.

Nevins, Allan. 1964. *Lincoln and the Gettysburg Address.* Commemorative Papers. Urbana: Univ. of Illinois Press.

Newcomb, Robert M. 1979. *Planning the Past.* Hamden, Conn.: Archon.

Niebuhr, Reinhold. 1964. "The Religion of Abraham Lincoln." In Allan Nevins, ed. *Lincoln and the Gettysburg Address.* Urbana: Univ. of Illinois Press, 72–87.

Olwig, Kenneth. 1984. *Natures' Ideological Landscape.* London: Allen and Unwin.

Oyler, John S. 1972. "Picket Charges: Everyone Else Pays: The Story of the Gettysburg Tower Controversy." Senior Thesis, Princeton University.

Penning-Rowsell, Edmund C. 1986. "Themes, Speculation and an Agenda for Landscape Research." In Edmund Penning-Rowsell and David Lowenthal, eds. *Landscape: Meanings and Values.* London: Allen and Unwin, 114–28.

Peterson, Charles E. 1931. Memo to National Park Service Director, May 29. National Park Service Records, National Archives Record Group 79.

Porter, Charles W. III. 1945. Memo to National Park Service. Director, July 13. Branch of History, Dept. of Int.

Quadrant Marketing Counselors Ltd. 1978. "America's Forgotten War: A Conceptual Program for Sackets Harbor—Madison Barracks." New York. Mimeo.

Rabinovitz, Francine F. 1974. "Types of Local Political Systems and Planning Policy." In W. D. Hawley and F. M. Wirt, eds. *The Search for Community Power.* Englewood Cliffs, N.J.: Prentice-Hall, 343–56.

Relph, Edward C. 1980. *Place and Placelessness.* London: Pion.

———. 1981. *Rational Landscapes and Humanistic Geography.* Beckenham, U.K.: Croom Helm.

———. 1984. "Seeing, Thinking, and Describing Landscapes." In Thomas F. Saarinen et al., eds. *Environmental Perception and Behavior.* Dept. of Geography, Univ. of Chicago, no. 209, 209–23.

Ricci David M. 1971. *Community Power and Democratic Theory: The Logic of Political Analysis.* New York: Random House.

Rowntree, Lester B. and Margerit W. Conkey. 1980. "Symbolism and the Cultural Landscape." *Annals, Association of American Geographers* 70 (4): 459–74.

Runte, Alfred. 1987. *National Parks: The American Experience.* Lincoln: Univ. of Nebraska Press.

Rushton, Gerard. 1984. "Maintaining the Fundamental Principles: A Commentary." In Thomas F. Saarinen et al., eds. *Environmental Perception and Behavior* Dept. of Geography, Univ. of Chicago, no. 209, 245–50.

Saarinen, Thomas F. 1976. *Environmental Planning: Perception and Behavior.* Prospect Heights, Ill.: Waveland Press.

Saarinen, Thomas F., D. Seamon, and J. L. Sell, eds. 1984. *Environmental Perception and Behavior: An Inventory and Prospect.* Dept. of Geography, Univ. of Chicago, no. 209.

Sadler, Barry, and Allen Carlson, eds. 1982. *Environmental Aesthetics: Essays in Interpretation.* Victoria: Western Geographical Series, no. 20.

St. Lawrence-Eastern Ontario Commission. 1985. *Village of Sackets Harbor Urban Cultural Management Plan.* Watertown, Pa.

Schlereth, Thomas J. 1980. *Artifacts and the American Past.* Nashville, Tenn.: American Association for State and Local History.

Serrin, William. 1986. "Away from Fast-Food Joints, Some Find a Special Gettysburg." *New York Times,* July 4 : 12.

Shabecoff, Philip. 1987. "U.S. Fights a New Battle of Antietam." *New York Times,* Nov. 10 : 12.

Shoemyen, Anne H., ed. 1987. *1987 Florida Statistical Abstract.* Gainesville: Univ. Presses of Florida.

Sitwell, O. F. G., and Oleuka S. E. Bilash. 1986. "Analyzing the Cultural Landscape as a Means of Probing the Non-material Dimension of Reality." *Canadian Geographer* 30 (2): 132–45.

Sloan, Eric. 1955. *Our Vanishing Landscape.* New York: Ballantine.

Smith, Ellen Harvie. 1939. Letter to R. Lee, July 10. National Archives Record Group 79.

Steele, Fritz. 1981. *The Sense of Place.* Boston: CBI Publishing.

Stilgoe, John R. 1982. *Common Landscapes of America, 1580–1845.* New Haven: Yale Univ. Press.

Tebeau, Charlton W. 1971. *A History of Florida.* Coral Gables: Univ. of Miami Press.

Terhune, F. W., ed. 1983. *Florida Statistical Abstract.* 17th ed. Gainesville: Univ. Presses of Florida.

Toth, Susan Allen. 1982. *Blooming: A Small-Town Girlhood.* Boston: Little, Brown.

——. 1984. *Ivy Days: Making My Way Out East.* Boston: Little Brown.

——. 1987. "The Importance of Being Remembered." *The New York Times Book Review,* June 28, Section B 1 : 37–38.

Trounstine, Philip J., and Terry Christensen. 1982. *Movers and Shakers: The Study of Community Power.* New York: St. Martins.

Tuan, Yi-Fu. 1974. *Topophilia: A Study of Environmental Perception, Attitudes, and Values.* Englewood Cliffs, N.J.: Prentice-Hall.

——. 1977. *Space and Place: The Perspective of Experience.* Minneapolis: Univ. of Minnesota Press.

Wagner, Philip L. 1974. "Cultural Landscapes and Regions: Aspects of Communication." In H. J. Walker and W. G. Haag, eds. *Man and Cultural Heritage.* Baton Rouge: School of Geosciences 5, 133–42.

Wallace McHarg Roberts, and Todd and Gladstone Associates. 1972. *Gettysburg-Cumberland Demonstration Program.* Harrisburg: Pennsylvania Dept. of Community Affairs.

Warner, W. Lloyd. 1959. *The Living and the Dead: A Study of the Symbolic Life of Americans.* New Haven: Yale Univ. Press.

Waste, Robert J., ed. 1986. *Community Power: Directions for Future Research.* Beverly Hills: Sage.

——. 1987. *Power and Pluralism in American Cities: Researching the Urban Laboratory.* New York: Greenwood.

Whitehand, J. W. R., ed. 1981. *The Urban Landscape: Historical Development and Management.* New York: Academic.

Williams, Norman, Jr., Edmund H. Kellogg, and Frank B. Gilbert. 1983. *Readings in Historic Preservation: Why? What? How?* New Brunswick, N.J.: Center for Urban Policy Research.

Williams, Raymond. 1973. *The Country and the City.* London: Oxford Univ. Press.

Wright, Frank Lloyd. 1938. "Wright Replies to Attacks on His Views." *Richmond Times-Dispatch,* November 6.

Yonge, Samuel H. 1907. *The Site of Old James Towne: 1607–1698.* Richmond: Hermitage Press.

Zelinsky, Wilbur. 1984. "O Say Can You See? Nationalistic Emblems in the Landscape" *Winterthur Portfolio* 19 (4): 277–86.

——. 1986. "The Changing Face of Nationalism in the American Landscape." *Canadian Geographer* 30 (2): 171–75.

Zube, Ervin H., Richard O. Brush, and Julius Gy. Fabos. 1975a. *Landscape Assessment: Values, Perceptions, and Resources.* Stroudsburg, Pa.: Dowden, Hutchinson and Ross.

Zube, Ervin H., David G. Pitt, and Thomas W. Anderson. 1975b. "Perceptions and Prediction of Scenic Resource Values of the Northeast." In Ervin Zube et al. 1975a. *Landscape Assessment: Values, Perceptions, and Resources.* Stroudsburg, Pa.: Dowden, Hutchinson and Ross, 151–67.

Index

America's Historic Landscapes was designed by Dariel Mayer, composed by G & S Typesetters, Inc., printed by Cushing-Malloy, Inc., and bound by John H. Dekker & Sons, Inc. The book is set in Trump Mediaeval, with Raleigh Bold used for display, and printed on 60-lb Glatfelter Antique, B-16.